American Oak Furniture

STYLES AND PRICES

BOOK III

ROBERT W. AND HARRIETT SWEDBERG

Other books by Robert W. and Harriett Swedberg:

American Oak Furniture Styles and Prices, Revised
American Oak Furniture Styles and Prices, Book II
Country Furniture and Accessories with Prices
Country Furniture and Accessories with Prices, Book II
Country Pine Furniture Styles and Prices, Revised
Country Store 'n' More
Furniture of the Depression Era
Off Your Rocker
Tins 'n' Bins
Victorian Furniture Styles and Prices, Revised
Victorian Furniture Styles and Prices Book II
Victorian Furniture Styles and Prices Book III
Wicker Furniture Styles and Prices

Cover design: Anthony Jacobson
Interior layout: Anthony Jacobson
Editor: Lynne Weatherman
Photography: Robert and Harriett Swedberg
Printing and Enlarging: Tom Luse

Library of Congress Catalog Card Number 87-50369

ISBN 0-87069-492-8

10 9 8 7 6 5 4 3 2

Published by

A Capital Cities/ABC, Inc. Company

Wallace-Homestead Book Company
201 King of Prussia Road
Radnor, Pennsylvania 19089

Contents

Foreword

Just as in previous editions, the Swedbergs again provide accurate, up-to-date values for antique American oak furniture, in an arresting and entertaining manner. The third edition of the *American Oak Furniture Styles and Prices* series is extravagantly illustrated with hundreds of photographs (including color) and is filled with useful information to help you in your oak furniture hunting.

Robert and Harriett Swedberg have traveled thousands of miles across the country to compile hundreds of current prices of American oak furniture. But this is more than just a price guide—along with new prices, you'll learn the interesting history behind the oak furniture you love. How do you tell the difference between *plain-sawn* and *quarter-sawn* oak, or a *pressed-back* and a *T-back* chair? Who led the Arts and Crafts Movement in America? What are the most common oak imitators, and how do you spot them?

Additionally, the Swedbergs have included supplemental reference sections—such as an oak furniture glossary and an easy-to-use index—to complete the book.

Whether you're a serious collector or a "Saturday browser," you need the most up-to-date, accurate price guide available for intelligent oak furniture buying. With many thousands of copies in print, *American Oak Furniture Styles and Prices Book III* is the best-selling expert you'll want by your side.

Acknowledgments

The authors sincerely thank the following collectors and dealers who freely gave of their time and knowledge to assist us in obtaining photographs and prices for this book. We also thank those who did not wish to be listed.

Ackerman's Newton Road Antiques
Bill and Karen Ackerman
Iowa City, Iowa

Antique Corner in the Yapp Building
Wayne and Audrey Yapp
Mt. Horeb, Wisconsin

Antiques in the Olde White Church
Jim and Judy Ball
Hills, Iowa

Antiques Mall of Madison
Madison, Wisconsin

Antiques Unlimited
Douglas and Marie Blair
Murfreesboro, Tennessee

Bloomington Antique Mall
Doug and Beverly Jennings
Bloomington, Illinois

Bob Adams Antique Mall
Bob and Karen Adams
Caledonia, Wisconsin

The Brenner Collection

Columbus Antique Mall and Museum
Norm and Virginia Hageman
Columbus, Wisconsin

Edward Conradt
Lincoln, Nebraska

Cottage Antiques
Janet Goetz
The Antique Mall
Iowa City, Iowa

Country Charm Antiques
Dan and Sandy Kitts
Lacon, Illinois

Country Parlor Antiques
Richard Lentz and Vivian Brzezinski
Janesville, Wisconsin

Dawson Antiques
Tom Dawson
Washington, Iowa

The Glass Case
Grace Jochimsen
The Antique Mall
Iowa City, Iowa

Grandma's Trunk
Audrey Miller
Grand River Merchants of Williamston
Williamston, Michigan

Philip Gregory
Illinois Antique Center
Peoria, Illinois

Hawk Antiques
Arnold and Shirley Hawk
St. Joseph, Illinois

Hoff Mall Antique Center
William Crawford
Mt. Horeb, Wisconsin

The Illinois Antique Center
Dan Philips
Peoria, Illinois

Kalona Antique Company
Ken and Brenda Herington
Kalona, Iowa

The Louisville Antique Mall
Harold L., Chuck, and Don Sego
Louisville, Kentucky

Melon City Antique Mart
Joe and Mary Cline
Muscatine, Iowa

Petersen's Antiques
Ron and Adrienne Petersen
Kimballton, Iowa

Brad, Jan, Ryan, and Sara Pierce

Ricklefs Antiques
Doug and Nancy Ricklefs
Anamosa, Iowa

School Days Antiques Mall and Specialty
Shops
Eric and Judy Sewell
Sturtevant, Wisconsin

Tom and Vicki Sneddon

Everett Sorenson

Vintage Books and Clothing
Joe and Pam Michaud
The Antique Mall
Iowa City, Iowa

Webb's Antique Mall
Verlon Webb
Centerville, Indiana

Yesterday Oncemore Antiques
Louise Anderson and Larry Crowder
Nashville, Tennessee

1
Where Did You Get *That* Price?

Owners' prices and influencing factors.

The pricing of furniture and accessories in this book was set by the dealers and collectors who own the pieces. Items are ready for home use unless otherwise stated.

As in our previous books, we have used a price tag policy. This means that the values listed under the pictures are those that were attached to the articles of furniture by the dealer or by the collector-owner.

We do not set prices. Please remember that this book is a guide to values only. Neither the publisher nor the authors assume responsibility for any losses that may incur as a result of using this book.

It's important to point out (especially to the novice) that many factors influence the price a dealer assigns to a piece of furniture. For example:

☐ Original price. How much did the dealer have to pay for the piece?
☐ Condition. Was the item in home-ready condition or did it need to be refinished, repaired, reupholstered, caned, or restored in any manner?

Before and after photographs of a Larkin combination bookcase-desk are shown on the following page. In the first photo, the bookcase-desk is shown at an auction house in its *as found* state. Notice that the pattern of the wood does not show up well. The bidder who took home this prize refinished it so that the grain is exposed to enhance its

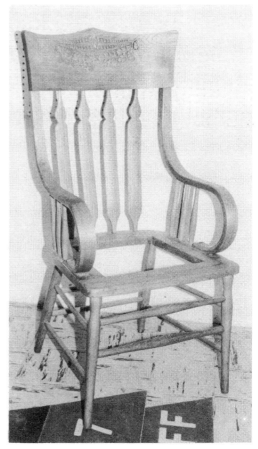

Ash pressed-back armchair; 23" arm to arm, 44" high. In Iowa, $125.

beauty. She bought the *side-by-side,* as it is currently called, for $600, but places an $800 value on it now.

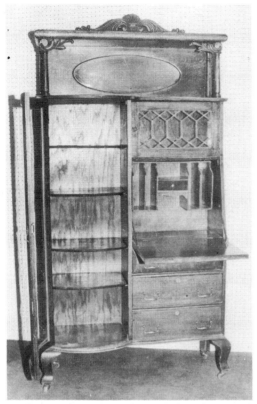

Larkin combination bookcase-desk with original label on the back; 40" wide, 14" deep, 73" high. In Iowa, $600.

The same Larkin combination bookcase-desk, shown in the previous picture, after it was refinished. In Iowa, $800.

Next, examine the ash armchair (shown on the previous page). It is seatless because the owner understands that home decors differ—that a prospective buyer might enjoy selecting his or her own fabrics and colors. Additionally, the cost of the labor and the material needed to redo the seat would be an extra expense to the seller. Thus, this chair is priced at $125.

Likewise, the oak love seat shown here is also seatless. Consequently, it has a $325 tag. Both pieces have been refinished and are ready to receive the proper coverings that the purchaser, not the dealer, feels are appropriate.

Other factors that influence the price of an item:

☐ Labor costs. Does the owner do his or her own work or must someone be hired to do it?

Love seat; 44" arm to arm, 20" deep, 41" high. In Iowa, $325.

☐ Overhead. For example, renting a store and paying the associated utilities in a tourist area or in a city generally costs more than the same amount of space in a small town or rural area. A shop within a home reduces the overhead considerably.

☐ Staff size. The number of employees on the staff adds to the expense.

☐ Availability and salability. For example, those who collect the straight-lined mission furniture consider it prestigious to own articles marked with the Gustav Stickley label—but these items are not always easy to locate.

☐ Marketability. Generally, in golden oak, a china cabinet is more marketable than a huge buffet that may be too large for a modern home. Then, too, some shoppers seek ornate furniture with grotesques, claw feet, curvatures, and carvings. This adds dollars to the price tag.

☐ Location. Some articles sell better in one area of the country than in another. This influences prices since supply and demand is a basic factor in retailing.

☐ Sentimentality. This tends to cause private owners to overvalue furniture that has been handed down in the family from generations past. Such pieces are literally impossible for a dealer to buy and market appropriately.

☐ Intact original. An antiquer's view of uniting two as one has a discordant, not a romantic connotation. When two mismatched parts are joined as a whole, the result is called a *marriage*. Such a combination is of lesser value than that of a complete, original piece of furniture.

The dealer who owns a kitchen cupboard of mixed woods will explain to potential purchasers that this unit is a marriage. As such, the dealer has priced it at $675. The original cupboard, with both the base and the top as manufactured, would be listed at $1,100, instead.

Two-piece kitchen cupboard (a marriage of an elm top and oak bottom); 44" wide, 79" high. In Iowa, $675.

Examine the photograph of the kitchen cupboard: The top is a combination of elm and ash with a scalloped design on the doors. Now look at the oak base. The doors are straight with applied diamonds in the center, and the base drawers have incised carving on them, but there is no like design on the top piece. The differences in the woods and the incompatabiltiy of the ornamentations are an obvious indication of a marriage.

The list could continue, but the important lesson to be learned is that a price guide is only that. It merely leads the way to help readers as they place values on their pieces.

2
Characteristics of Oak and Its Look-Alikes

Sawing differences and five resemblers.

Did You Know?

☐ *Annual rings* are a tree's concentric seasonal growth layers inside the tree trunk. These bull's-eye-like circles can easily be seen on a stump or the base of a log where it is severed from the tree.

☐ *Pores* are small openings for the discharge and absorption of fluids. When pores can readily be seen, as in oak, the wood is referred to as *open-grained.*

Closed-grained means the pores are more difficult to observe. In some species, you may even require the help of a magnifying glass to detect the pores' presence. Since open-grained woods accept stain readily, oak can be golden hued, darkly fumed through the use of ammonia vapors, or stained as desired.

☐ *Grain* is the arrangement and direction of fibers in wood that give the different species of wood their characteristic textures, markings, and patterns.

☐ *Medullary* or *pith rays* radiate from the center of a tree, almost in the way a small child draws a yellow sun ball with straight lines branching out around it. These cross the annual rings. Oak's pith rays are the largest found in any tree native to the United States, and are so pronounced that they're referred to as *flakes.*

☐ *Plain-sawed* or *sawn* indicates that boards are cut from the whole log, lengthwise in parallel sections at right angles to the rays. On oak, a pattern of stripes and elliptical *V*s results.

Plain-sawed oak jelly cupboard; 41" wide, 17" deep, 54" high. In Iowa, $595.

☐ *Quarter-sawed* or *sawn*, in early lumbering days, meant the log was cut in half lengthwise. Each half was then cut in half again. This cutting formed four equal rounded-end triangles (pie shaped wedges) that were sliced parallel to the rays and across the growth rings.

This method exposes oak's flakes (pith or medullary rays) to demonstrate a pronounced pattern in the resulting planks.

Today, some people see these large rays or flakes and imaginatively picture them as stripes on a tiger. To these observers, it seems appropriate to call the quarter-sawed wood *tiger oak*. Because the process of quarter-sawing wastes wood and requires more processing, it is less expensive to plain-saw lumber. However, quarter-sawed oak shrinks and warps less than the plain-sawed variety.

Remarkably, 60 varieties of oak trees are indigenous to the United States. Approximately 14 of these are used by the home furnishings industry, but white oak, with its strength, beauty, and durability is the primary oak of choice. Red oak, too, is widely used. Generally, the oak found in the manufacture of furniture comes from the area east of the Great Plains.

There are always certain "it has to be included" elements and terms in a book about furniture. For instance, there is no precise date or time at which one style of furniture or one type of wood ceases to be desired and another becomes very popular, so the word *circa* (*about*) proves helpful to us—it indicates approximate time periods for when certain pieces were made and were in high demand.

Oak As a Furniture Wood

Oak has long been used as a furniture wood. *Jacobean* furniture with its twisted turnings and ornamental carvings was prevalent in England circa 1603–1688. This style experienced a reincarnation around the 1870s in the United States, but was not widely accepted. (Black walnut, used extensively from circa 1840 through the end of the century, was still King of the Woods.) After America's virgin walnut forest began to be depleted, circa 1880, light-in-color oak became the style queen. Since these trees grew prolifically on the North American continent, they were readily available to lumber companies. Since then, oak consistently has been one of the main furniture woods.

This does not mean that back in the 1800s oak and woods with similar characteristics (such as ash) were ever completely

Quarter-sawed oak combination bookcase-desk with convex glass door and swell front top drawer; 37" wide, 12" deep, 70" high. In Wisconsin, $925.

vacant from the scene. While these did not dominate, they were continually present. Here is one illustration to substantiate this fact.

An 1873 catalogue from a furniture factory in Grand Rapids, Michigan, the 1800s Furniture Capital of the World, advertised specific household furnishings as being available in ash or walnut. A plain four-drawer ash bureau with no *decks* (generally called handkerchief boxes now) could be purchased for $6.25. The cost of its more-expensive walnut counterpart rated an additional 75 cents. Pine or poplar with a country flair; oak; and some maple, cherry, and mahogany, as well as other woods, coexisted with walnut in the 1800s when the latter wood was dominant.

While black walnut consistently is dark in hue, oak is more versatile. It is naturally endowed with a light-colored appearance, but can be treated to take on different tones. As a consequence, there are various finishes found on oak from the late 1800s and early 1900s. When orange shellac was applied, often with pigments added, the result was called *golden oak.* It was described in advertisements as "highly polished" or with a "high-gloss golden finish."

A certain dark appearance was inspired by tobacco chewers and spitters. The tale is told that David W. Kendall, one of the first furniture designers employed at a Grand Rapids, Michigan factory, was scoffed at by his competitors when he developed an antique oak finish. These men snickered and called this brownish look *mud.*

They did not realize that Kendall was intrigued by the stains tobacco spit caused. As he walked through the factory, he noticed that the bulging-mouthed workmen who chewed tobacco didn't always hit the spittoons with their wads. The oak floors darkened where the tobacco landed, and the result resembled *patina,* the natural deepening of wood after years of exposure to light, air, and dirt. Kendall began to experiment with a tobacco solution applied to wood, but when he failed to develop a lasting stain, he turned to a chemical concoction and achieved the result he desired. When furniture with this new finish sold well, his rivals quit chuckling and hastened to emulate this finish. *Antique oak* was in the furniture fashion spotlight.

Another man who was interested in finishes observed that the absorbing qualities of oak's large pores was increased by wetting its surface. Because of this, manufacturer and designer Gustav Stickley placed his assembled furniture in an airtight area with containers of strong ammonia. These containers of ammonia released a vapor that was allowed to penetrate the wood for a time period of up to two days, depending on the degree of darkness desired. Following the use of abrasive paper for smoothness, the surface was finished in either light or dark brown, or a silver gray. Stickley liked the resulting patina look.

A different way to fume oak was suggested in an article in the March 1912 issue of *Women's Home Companion,* a magazine published by Crowell Publishing Company. The article stated that while furniture could be placed in a kiln filled with burning straw, a more practical and less expensive procedure was to apply a hand-rubbed finish that the author claimed was preferable and more enduring.

Oak can be fancy. Golden oak furniture features pressed and/or carved designs. Frequently, the designs are fashioned independently and applied to a piece. Turnings, pillars, grotesque figures, heads of people, paw or claw feet, incised carvings, French legs, and other embellishments adorn bedroom suits, dining room pieces, parlor seats, and hall furnishings.

Oak can also be plain. Mission furniture (see Chapter 10) is stoic and straight, often with distinctive large hardware, obvious mortise and tenon joinings, and unadorned wooden uprights. It is strong and pure of line. Both the plain mission and the fancy golden oak were much sought after as the stylish furnishings in the homes of the early 1900s.

Oak and Look-Alikes

Did you realize that oak is one of six look-alikes? In addition to this large tree that grows from an acorn, the sextet includes ash, chestnut, elm, hickory, and artificial graining applied to an inexpensive base wood. Each one of these woods deserves a further description, as they share some characteristics with oak.

Ash. Since the grain of ash and oak resemble each other, many old-time "oak" iceboxes, currently being sold, are really ash. Early 1900 catalogues advertised refrigerators (iceboxes) made of Northern ash or elm. Entire bedroom suits of the late 1800s were occasionally fashioned from ash. Because oak has a tendency to crack, the more resilient ash is used for sports equipment, including baseball bats, tennis racquets, and skis. Bent parts such as bows or hoop backs on chairs are frequently made of this wood because it bends with ease.

Ash and elm parlor table; 28" square, 39" high. In Illinois, $115.

Chestnut bureau washstand; 32" wide, 18" deep, 32" high with a 6" back rail. In Wisconsin, $225.

Chestnut. Chestnut is softer (not so tough as oak) and has a coarse, open grain, but lacks oak's large medullary rays. It is good for the hidden parts in drawer construction and as a core for veneering. It resists warping. Picture frames, woodwork, and paneling are constructed of chestnut. In some instances, chestnut is united with oak

Ash fall-front secretary; 36" wide, 18" deep, 85" high. In Wisconsin, $1,685.

to form case pieces. This wood is not too plentiful since many wild chestnut trees succumbed to a blight in the early 1900s.

Elm. Elm has an oak-like texture, bends well, and does not split readily, making it suitable for curved parts such as hoop backs on chairs. Elm, with its pleasing figure, unfortunately has a tendency to warp. However, these two combined characteristics make it a good candidate for veneer work— its beauty can be preserved and the warping tendency controlled through application as a thin layer over another surface.

Elm swivel desk chair; 25" arm to arm, 47" high. In Wisconsin, $345.

Bentwood (these parts were often made of ash, elm, or hickory) pressed cane-back platform rocker with upholstered seat; 21" arm to arm, 32" high. In Illinois, $325.

Many "oak" iceboxes are actually elm, as are some bedroom chests. This means that elm was used not only for veneers, but for solid pieces of furniture, too.

A good example of elm is included in Chapter 1 under the photograph of a two-piece *marriage cupboard.*

Hickory. Hickory shares oak's color and texture. It is supple, tough, and strong, but also slightly splintery and hard to work. Despite this, it does bend well. When strength and thickness are both required, hickory meets the need. For this reason, in colonial times, it was selected for the larger bent parts of furniture.

Oak. Oak is light in color, durable, hard, coarse, and has large pores. Its very distinct pith or medullary rays, called *flakes,* show vividly when the lumber is quarter-sawed. Stripes and elliptical *V*'s are usually apparent in plain-sawed oak. Since oak

doesn't readily rot, a table stored for years in a damp basement may weather the ordeal without the legs greatly deteriorating. Other woods do not fair so well in high humidity environments.

Artificial Grain. In the late 1800s and early 1900s, less expensive, nondescript light woods were stroked with special brushes, combs, patterned rollers, or other graining devices. By this bit of skillful trickery, an oak-like countenance appeared.

In 1897, a bedroom suit with an unspecified wood origin was available finished in antique oak. Sears Roebuck sold such sets for $10.50. Its "elegant solid oak" counterpart wore a $16 price tag.

This deception of disguising a humble wood enabled fashion-conscious people of limited means to purchase fake oak at an affordable price.

Detecting Fake Oak

It is possible to detect artificial graining over a solid wood. Wear signs offer assistance. Examine the places where hands frequently touch the furniture. Are chair arms minus some grain where human arms moist with perspiration rubbed across them continually? Are there worn spots present around door or drawer pulls? Is the "oak" pattern fading out on the top where objects were moved about?

Look for wood that matches. For example, on a table, check beneath to determine whether both the top and its underside have similar characteristics. The same principle works on case pieces such as dressers or chests. An inspection of both sides of the top, in order to note any variation, is possible by removing the uppermost drawer. In addition, a solid-wood drawer front should have similar grain characteristics on both sides.

Be aware that fake oak grain will disappear if you apply paint remover to its surface. You may end up with an attractive lightwood piece without its oak coat. This new look however, in the opinion of many collectors, can have a charm of its own.

Finishing Oak Furniture

A finish helps protect wood from damage. For example, if a damp glass is set on an untreated wooden surface for a period of time, the moisture has an opportunity to penetrate the fibers. When this happens, a black ring results.

The authors of this book find the lasting qualities of multiple coats of a hand-rubbed

Artificially grained (to imitate quarter-sawed oak) C-roll-top metal desk of the 1930s; 60" wide, 36" deep, 45" high. In Kentucky, $1,395.

satin sheen varnish to be a durable and attractive finish. Such a surface withstands heat, water, and alcohol damage well, and will not develop an alligator or crazed finish after years of use.

Shellac, lacquer, and specially prepared commercial or hand-mixed solutions concocted by individuals themselves, are the choices of others. Besides serving to preserve and polish the wood, properly applied coatings enhance the surface's beauty.

Whether you like your oak furniture plain or fancy, light or dark, or in an oak look-alike concept, this book shows you many pieces that are available on today's market. Although none of the photographs used in this book are from museums, many are of that caliber. Don't lose sight of the fact that those desirable dressers, desks, tables, and other oak pieces are still out there if you keep searching. Happy hunting!

3
An Attractive Entry

*Hall trees, mirrors, and
benches.*

Did you know?

☐ An *applied carving* is crafted separately
and attached to a piece of furniture.

☐ A *molding* is a shaped strip of wood used
for ornamental purposes.

☐ A *pediment* is a horizontal decorative feature mounted on the top of a tall piece of
furniture. It is often curved in a *scroll* or
arch shape.

☐ A *grotesque* is a figure, or parts of figures,
of people or animals intermixed with foliage, fruits, or flowers in an unnatural
manner.

☐ *Paw feet* on furniture received that name
because they look like an animal's paws.

☐ *Beading* is a type of molding with raised
shapes that resemble beads.

Past generations referred to the hall at
the entrance of a modern home as a *vesti-
bule.* This hallway is a home's silent greeter.
When it is cheerful, interesting, and attractive, it seems to welcome people, inviting
them to come in.

Before guest closets were prevalent in
the entrance hall, the *hall tree* or *hall rack*
was an important utilitarian item. A common version consisted of a tall standing
frame with a series of hooks for hanging
outer garments such as hats, coats, scarves,
or stoles.

*Hall tree with lift-lid storage compartment, bev-
eled mirror, wooden umbrella holders, and metal
drip pans; 33" wide, 14" deep, 77" high. In Indiana, $350.*

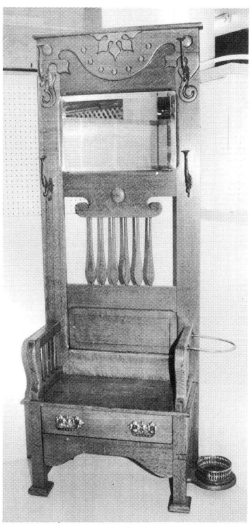

Hall tree with drawer in bench base, beveled mirror, brass umbrella holder, and metal drip pan; 29" wide, 16" deep, 80" high. In Illinois, $795.

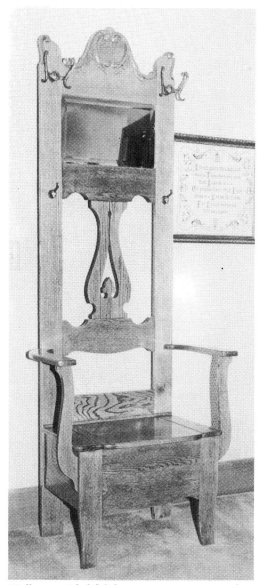

Hall tree with lift-lid storage compartment, beveled mirror; 30" wide, 16" deep, 78" high. In Iowa, $400.

A mirror for adjusting hair or hats was helpful, as was a bench on which to sit while removing or donning overshoes. If this seat had a hinged lid over a storage box, the hall tree had an additional function. Depending on the family's needs, this area was a hideout for articles such as boots, scarves, and mittens. Some versions had drawers that served similar purposes.

Usefulness of the hall rack was increased when arms circled out to hold erect rain-drenched umbrellas. Removable metal pans, frequently with cast designs or ornamental shapes, such as a shell formation, were at the base to catch any drips.

If the hall rack was ponderous or top heavy, it was attached to the wall to keep it from falling forward. An examination of photographs shows hall trees with different characteristics, including moldings or applied decorations, and one is crowned on top by a pediment. If such a rack proved to be overpowering in a small entryway, a mirror with hooks in its surrounding frame could function as a hat and coat receiver.

Hall tree with lift-lid storage compartment, metal umbrella holder, and beveled mirror; 28" wide, 14" deep, 75" high. In Illinois, $675.

Larkin hall tree with lift-lid storage compartment, beveled mirror, and tag, which reads in part: "If you have occasion to write to us about its condition, use Factory No. 12 for quick reply. Larkin Co., Buffalo, N.Y."; 28" wide, 19" deep, 76" high. In Wisconsin, $495.

Hall hat-and-coat mirror with beveled mirror; 47" wide, 26" high. In Wisconsin, $185.

Hall hat-and-coat mirror with six brass hooks; 34" wide, 22" high. In Iowa, $110.

Hall bench with lift-lid storage compartment, paw feet, and grotesque open-mouth heads on arms and back panel; 46" wide, 18" deep, 43" high. In Iowa, $750.

Hall tree with lift-lid storage compartment, beveled mirror, and applied decorations near and on pediment top; 27" wide, 16" deep, 78" high. In Ohio, $495.

Creative modern housewives no longer restrict these pieces to hall duty. The furnishings with hooks serve in the bathroom as towel holders or as a place to hang garments during a shower. A lift lid becomes a hideaway for toilet supplies.

A separate hall bench frequently stood with its back to the wall, and its hinged seat doubled as a storage compartment. A set resulted when a framed mirror of like wood and a comparable design hung on the wall above the bench.

Notice the bench with the grotesque in the center of the back panel. The seat's short legs terminate in paw feet. A molding tops this example, and applied carving shows well on the arms. One illustrated bench has various decorative features, including beading, both applied and incised carving, and paw feet.

Hall bench with drawer, paw feet, beading, applied and pressed decorations; 44" wide, 19" deep, 44" high. In Illinois, $525.

Hall benches, when moved out of their intended habitats, provide additional seating anywhere in the house. This is especially true when country-oriented pillow animals or fowls, fashioned from salvaged pieces of worn quilts or coverlets, adorn their surfaces. These worn bed covers are called *cutters* by the trade and are sold for such projects.

4
A Place to Sit

Benches, stools, parlor suits, chairs, and rocking chairs.

Did You Know?

☐ *Diner* is a late-1800s/early-1900s catalogue name for a dining room chair. Nonetheless, the term *dining room chair* appeared simultaneously.

☐ *Heavily carved* or *embossed chairs* are illustrated in passé catalogues. Today, the terminology has changed, and they are called *pressed backs.*

☐ *Pressed backs* on chairs resulted when a machine stamped into the wood a shallow pattern that was intended to resemble hand carving. Chairs with double-, triple-, or quadruple-pressed designs are available.

☐ *T-back* is the modern term for chairs with backs that resemble a printed capital *T,* in configuration.

☐ *Cane chairs* can be made by hand with strands of rattan woven through holes that surround the seat frame. When grooves encircling the chair seat are present, prewoven sheets of cane are forced into them and glued tightly in place with a spline cover. This forms a *pressed cane seat.*

☐ *Patented seats* include highchairs that convert to rockers or go-carts. Patented platform rockers of different types offer secure seats for those who distrust the tilting and creeping characteristics of ordinary rockers.

☐ *Bentwood* furniture was created by Michael Thonet in Vienna, Austria in about 1840.

Bench from Murray County, Tennessee courthouse; 57" wide, 23" deep, 36" high. In Tennessee, $365.

☐ *Fainting couch* is the present-day term for an elongated, backless seat, with a rolled pillow at one end upon which one could sit or lie down. Old catalogues refer to it as a *couch.*

☐ A *bed lounge* resembled a couch with a back added. In addition, it opened to provide a sleeping surface.

When you think of furnishing a home, comfort is a primary consideration. Because of this, it's important to decide what type of seating arrangements will serve you best. Benches meet various needs, and their place in the home differs. Often, they accompany tables in small eating areas. Frequently, they're pulled up near the fireplace where sitters become entranced by the multicolored flames.

Cane-seat pressed-back chair; 41" high. In Wisconsin, $325 for a set of two.

Cane-seat pressed- and cut-back chair; 38" high. In Iowa, $390 for a set of three.

Next of kin to benches are stools. One woman, who displays her antiques and collectibles at large flea markets, says Chicago suburbanites like stools and will grab any she brings before she can unload her truck completely. Neither of these forms represents the apex of comfort, however. For more easy sitting, consider the dining room first.

Catalogues from the late 1800s and early 1900s advertised *heavily carved* or *embossed diners,* or more explicitly, dining room chairs. Despite this, many of the decorations on chair slats were not actually carved. Instead, a metal die machine with an engraved design stamped a pattern, which resembled hand carving, into the wood fibers to create the shallow embossed look.

Heat, extreme pressure, and the quality of the die itself helped achieve a carved appearance. If chiseling or cutting provided an additional accent, a more deeply embossed effect resulted. These latter touches please specialized collectors who realize that this additional workmanship increases the value of such chairs.

Chairs with double-, triple-, or quadruple-pressed designs on back slats and/or on the apron under the seat are available. While examples with only the embossed top rail abound, multipressed styles appear with less frequency. A premium price ordinarily is paid for those with more than a single pressing.

Cane-seat Man-of-the-Wind double-pressed-back chair; 42" high. In Illinois, $960 for a set of four.

Close-up of Man-of-the-Wind pressed back.

Flowers, garlands, and scrolls are common, while designs such as fish or grotesques are rare. Currently, dealers refer to a chubby faced man with his mouth posed as if he is blowing out air as a "Man-of-the-Wind." Chairs with unusual designs such as this command a higher price than their more easily obtained counterparts.

Since matched sets of chairs are more costly, some people purchase individual pressed-back chairs that are similar in contour and height. This purposeful mismatching is a budget-minded manner in which to obtain the desired number of chairs—4, 6, or 8—even though they do not form a coordinated set.

Other purchasers with economical traits are buying T-backs. A few years ago T-backs were inexpensive—collectors coveted the pressed backs. Since pressed-backed chairs are now costly and difficult to acquire in sets, the price of T-backs has increased.

How did the diners, with their squarish seats described in catalogues as *box seated chairs*, experience a name change to *T-back chairs?* These chairs feature a single perpendicular splat crossed at the top by a straight horizonatal slat. Present-day owners were reminded of the twentieth letter of the alphabet and dubbed them *T-backs.* Even with slight variations in their contours, the back does resemble a printed capital *T.* In addition to the pressed and T-formations, other backs feature odd shapes, turned spindles, or veneered surfaces.

Chair seats vary greatly. Some have cane bottoms that are handwoven through holes which have been drilled in a continuous line around the large hole in the middle of the seat's wooden frame. Another type of cane is purchased in prewoven sheets and is cut to fit the empty space in the seat. The ends are pulled straight and taut, and are fit and glued into an incised groove that circles the gap. The woven sheets are held securely by measured pieces of spline that are forced into the router lines.

T-back chair with upholstered seat; 37" high. In Iowa, $200 for a set of four.

Cane-seat chair with veneered and pressed back; 39" high. In Tennesee, $595 for a set of four.

In addition to the two types of cane bottoms, dining room chairs are available with solid wood, leather, pseudo leather, upholstered seats, cobbler seats of sturdy embossed fiber, or slip seats that can be removed when recovering is necessary. Shoppers at the turn of the century were offered selections just like those offered to present-day buyers who examine the merchandise available in antiques shops.

A later-style chair was a *dinette* or *breakfast type.* Many had brightly colored or black stenciled designs on their surfaces. Others were stained or painted. Generally, they accompanied tables with similar decorations to form dinette or breakfast sets. These small-size groupings were popular in the 1920s, 1930s, and 1940s. Recently, they have come back in favor.

Patriotic motifs have allure, and those with World War II emblems help date articles. The dinette or breakfast set pictured in this chapter (consisting of four chairs and a table with two self-storing leaves) is post-1942. An American Eagle with white touches is embossed on the back of each chair. Beneath the eagle is a blue applied *V.* This signifies the victory symbol that Great Britain's World War II Prime Minister, Sir Winston Churchill, presented to crowds when he raised two widespread fingers. A red star and blue incised *V* on the table corners complete the red, white, and blue theme on the limed oak set. (*Limed oak* denotes a bleached appearance, sometimes achieved through the use of a chlorinated lime solution.)

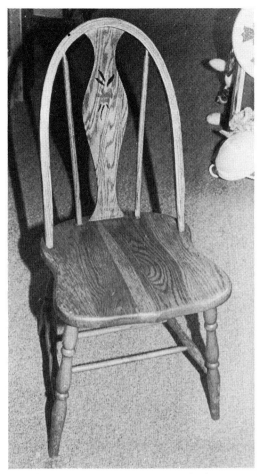

Wooden seat chair of the 1920s; 36" high. In Wisconsin, $125 for a set of four.

Cane-seat Mother Goose pressed-back highchair; 42" high. In Wisconsin, $200.

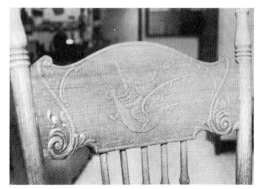

Close-up of Mother Goose pressed back.

Children's chair styles emulate those of their elders. Highchairs frequently have pressed designs on their backs. Ordinary highchairs from this era provided a safe place for a youngster to eat. They were available with or without tables (or *trays,* as they are more commonly called).

One of the photographs shows a signed Thonet bentwood highchair. Michael Thonet created bentwood furniture in Vienna, Austria around 1840. Soon this style was being successfully mass produced. Its designer felt that it was strong, functional, and aesthetically pleasing.

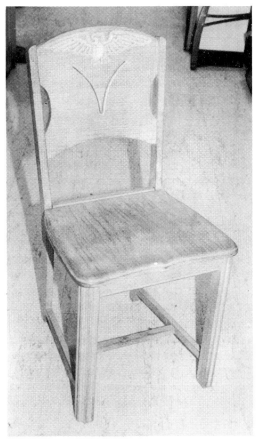

Wooden seat chair with impressed eagle and V on the back. Part of a set of four chairs and an extension table from the 1940s; 35" chair height; table 48" wide, 33" deep, 30" high. In Wisconsin, $235 for the five-piece set.

Cane-back and seat bentwood highchair, signed "Thonet"; 16" wide at tray, 37" high. In Iowa, $275.

Because patent furniture was a part of the late 1800s and early 1900s scene, babies had their own convertibles—highchairs that switched positions. While assorted combinations were possible, a chair that was kept at maximum height during meals could be readjusted and lowered afterward to form either a rocking chair or a go-cart.

In the past, more conventional rocking chairs could be purchased in child size, and now, all types of these chairs are once again being sought. Grandparents like them for their grandchildren. Doll and teddy bear enthusiasts display favorite collectibles in them. There are even indoor swings that became rocking chairs for tiny tots.

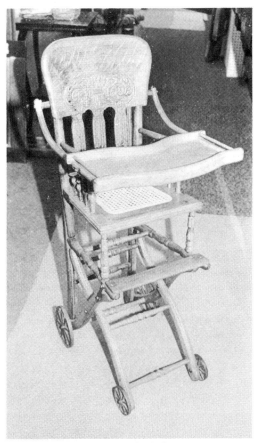

Cane-seat pressed-back highchair/go-cart combination, patented May 12, 1909; 41" high. In Wisconsin, $375.

Highchair/go-cart combination; 37" high. In Iowa, $325.

In the late 1800s and early 1900s, rocking chairs proved to be relaxing, and as a consequence, there are many varieties on the market today. While walnut and maple types are in generous supply, Victorian Era oak chairs, from the mid-1800s, with both cane backs and seats are rare. (A photograph of such a chair is included in this section.) There are numerous examples with only the seat caned—these were customarily made to accomodate a lady's dainty size.

Rockers of more generous proportions accommodated masculine frames. Ones with veneered rolled seats are apt to have some of the veneer chipped or pulled off. This detracts from their appearance and causes the prices of these to diminish accordingly. With their wide arms and spaciousness, manly rocking chairs can be comfortable, especially when the back slat or spindles curve slightly to conform to the body's contours.

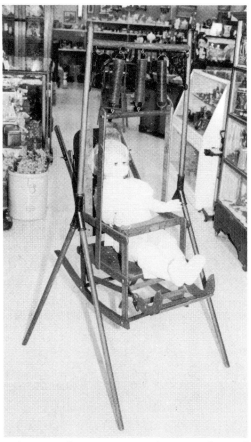

*Late 1800s Lincoln-type rolled-arm rocker; 21"
arm to arm, 39" high. In Kentucky, $145.*

*Baby swing that converts to rocker, manufactured
by Glascock Bros. Mfg. Co., Muncie, Ind., USA;
In Wisconsin, $400.*

Not everyone appreciates rocking
chairs. An occupant may fear that the rocker
will tip over backwards and forcefully eject
the sitter. Newspaper accounts from years
ago occasionally reported that an individual
sustained injuries from rocking off a porch
on a hot summer night. These accidents
were caused because such chairs have a tendency to creep across the floor when rocking. Too, rockers occasionally cut rugs or
help promote wear on them, and this de-
structive tendency displeases fastidious
homemakers.

Perhaps to overcome these obstacles,
different companies acquired patents on
platform rockers that would move back and
forth on a frame, or just had springs to produce motion. These platform rockers were

*Rocker with upholstered seat; 24" arm to arm, 34"
high. In Iowa, $120.*

Cane-seat double-pressed-back rocker; 40" high. In Wisconsin, $110.

Platform rocker with upholstered seat and back; 25" arm to arm, 37" high. In Wisconsin, $275.

Armchair with upholstered seat and back panel, spiral twist legs and spindles; 25" arm to arm, 39" high. In Illinois, $150.

Veneered back rocker with applied decorations; 23" arm to arm, 36" high. In Illinois, $185.

acceptable to sitters who disliked conventional versions. They gave the users a secure feeling and were less apt to damage carpets. Owners like to check metal portions to try to find enscribed patent dates. Such dates indicate that a particular chair was made in or after that year. The platform rockers' presence was noted especially between 1890 and 1915. At its inception, it was known as a *patent rocker*.

Move from the foyer into the parlor and imaginatively examine its 1897 decor. By mail-order shopping in a catalogue, it was possible to purchase a five-piece upholstered suit consisting of a large sofa, an easy platform rocker, a roomy easy arm-chair, and two straight parlor chairs. Carved wood was exposed on the chair arms, aprons, and backs. All of this luxury cost a total of $11.35 when upholstered with an inexpensive fabric.

Love seat with upholstered seat and back panels and applied decorations on rail and splat; 36" arm to arm, 23" deep, 40" high. In Wisconsin, $195.

*Combination bookcase-desk with beveled mirror, convex glass door, applied decorations, and claw feet; 38"
wide, 11" deep, 74" high. In Illinois, $895.*

Gustav Stickley #369 bent-arm reclining chair with original laced-leather seat; 33" arm to arm, 38" deep, 41" high. In Missouri, $4,950.

Roycroft bookstand with 14 volumes of Little Journeys *by Elbert Hubbard, Copyright 1916 by Roycrofters. Keyed tenon construction and marked Roycroft on a diamond-shaped metal tag on the side of the shoe foot; 26" wide, 14" deep, 26" high. In Iowa, $250.*

Gustav Stickley sewing chair (referred to as Thornden rocker) in dark fumed oak with rush seat, circa 1901; 31" high. In Illinois, $450.

Gustav Stickley #815 two-door china cabinet (painted blue inside) showing Harvey Ellis' influence with sloping top rail and arches at base; 39" wide, 15" deep, 64" high. In the Midwest, $4,500.

Gustav Stickley #212 V-back settle made between 1907 and 1912 with original hard leather seat and both the red decal and paper label; 47" arm to arm, 24" deep, 36" high. In Ohio, $2,500.

Gustav Stickley #922 full-sized bed with both paper and black burnt labels; 59" wide, headboard 55" high, footboard 46"high. In Nebraska, $5,000.

Elm and ash commode washstand with towel bar and serpentine top drawer; 34" wide, 19" deep, 53" high. In Iowa, $275.

Knock-down wardrobe with two full-length beveled mirrors, applied decorations, and two parallel drawers at base; 45" wide, 18" deep, 90" high. Dressing table chair with finger hold, applied decorations, and twist legs; 40" high. In Illinois, wardrobe $1,695; chair $195.

Round pedestal extension-table with claw feet and two 10" leaves; 54" diameter, 30" high. Cane-seat pressed- and carved-back chairs; 40" high. In Illinois, table $1,595; set of six chairs $1,350.

Corner china cabinet with two convex side doors, applied decorations, and two shelves near the top; 41" wide, 21" deep, 70" high. In Michigan, $2,500.

China sideboard with large beveled mirror in lower section, plain mirrors at top, applied decorations, and a grotesque at the center of top rail; 48" wide, 19" deep, 78" high. In Illinois, $1,895.

Cane-seat quadruple-pressed-back rocker; 38" high. In Iowa, $275.

Platform rocker with rolled-veneer seat and veneer back; 27" arm to arm, 38" high. In Iowa, $195.

33

S-roll-top desk with wooden pulls. Made by the Shelbyville Desk Co., Shelbyville, Indiana; 60" wide, 34" deep, 53" high. In Illinois, $5,950.

Rocker with incised designs on uprights, apron, and back; 28" arm to arm, 38" high. In Wisconsin, $135.

Couch (often called fainting couch*); 78" wide, 29" deep. In Wisconsin, $290.*

Bench with lift-lid storage compartment; 41" wide, 18" deep, 38" high. In Kentucky, $250.

If furniture construction was better, a higher grade material was used, and a matching *divan* (small sofa) was included, the price of the suit soared to $18.50. Elaborately carved and covered suits were also more costly. Parlor furniture representative of that from the late 1800s through the early decades of the 1900s is pictured in this chapter.

Actually, there were *overstuffed parlor suits* marketed in the 1890s, but families tended to discard the worn, outmoded sofas and chairs of that type, while saving the stiffer, straighter ones made with oak or birch frames. These are retrieved by delighted oak devotees today.

A descriptive phrase, evidently modern, is the term *fainting couch*. It refers to an elongated, backless seat with a rolled pillow at one end. A person could sit or lie down on it. The fainting couch conjours up a picture of a stereotyped helpless heroine of nineteenth century novels, who weakly collapses when faced with a crisis. She would often

Hall bench with applied decorations and lift-lid storage comparment. Originally, the base section of a large hall tree; 40" wide, 18" deep, 32" high. In Illinois, $375.

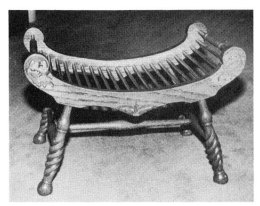

Bench; 24" wide, 14" deep, 16" high. In Iowa, $110.

Bench; 22" wide, 12" deep, 17" high. In Iowa, $110.

Bench; 24" wide, 14" deep, 20" high. In Wisconsin, $76.

carry her smelling salts and could faint away on the couch in a spectacularly pathetic, yet genteel, heap.

Catalogues of that day called these seats *couches*. A *bed lounge* differed because it opened to provide sleeping space in a hide-a-bed fashion. The bed lounge seat resembled that of a couch, but it had a back, usually with an upholstered section enclosed in a wooden frame.

The last pages of this chapter are devoted to the various types of seats available. Even though your items may differ from the ones photographed, the pictures may help lead you to an appreciation of their general value. These pieces are all in room-ready condition unless otherwise stated.

Piano or organ stool with metal claw and glass-ball feet; 14" diameter, 19" high in down position. In Illinois, $65.

36

Piano or organ stool with ice cream chair type base; 14" diameter, 18" high in high position. In Illinois, $60.

Cane-seat single-pressed-back chair; 39" high. In Wisconsin, $1,290 for a set of six.

Cane-seat single-pressed-back chair; 40" high. In Wisconsin, $450 for a set of four.

37

Cane-seat double-pressed-back chair, 42" high. In Iowa, $2,000 for a set of ten.

T-back chair with "leatherette" seat; 39" high. In Wisconsin, $199 for a set of four.

Carved-back love seat with upholstered seat and back; 34" arm to arm, 38" high. In Illinois, $425.

Wooden-seat chair; 36" high. In Iowa, $600 for a set of eight.

Cane-seat chair; 19" arm to arm, 45" high. In Wisconsin, $185.

Love seat with upholstered seat and back; 38" arm to arm, 22" deep, 36" high. In Iowa, $250.

Woven cane-seat chair; 43" high. In Illinois, $70.

Spindle-back chair with upholstered seat; 38" high. In Illinois, $275 for a set of four.

Side chair with upholstered seat; 34" high. In Wisconsin, $62.50.

T-back highchair; 18" arm to arm, 19" deep, 39" high. In Wisconsin, $75.

Cane-seat single-pressed-back highchair/go-cart combination, marked Wait Chair Co., 1903; 41" high. In Wisconsin, $425.

Pressed- and carved-back rocker with upholstered seat; 37" high. In Iowa, $225.

Cane-seat settee; 47" arm to arm, 18" deep, 38" high. In Kentucky, $495.

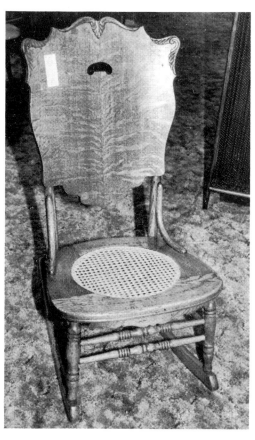

Cane-seat rocker with quarter-sawed back; 39" high. In Wisconsin, $130.

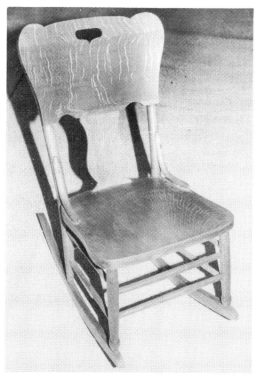

Rocker with finger hold; 32" high. In Illinois, $85.

Child's rocker with quarter-sawed veneered back;
15" arm to arm, 30" high. In Wisconsin, $45.

Child's pressed-back rocker with pressed design on
splat, made by Stomps Burkhardt Co., Dayton,
Ohio; 21" arm to arm, 32" high. In Indiana, $130.

Wooden seat single-pressed-back rocker; 28" arm to arm, 39" high. In Iowa, $195.

Side chair with quarter-sawed oak back and finger hold; 37" high. In Wisconsin, $280 for a set of four.

Veneered seat triple-pressed-back rocker; 25" arm to arm, 44" high. In Illinois, $185.

Cane-seat triple-pressed-back rocker; 24" arm to arm, 43" high. In Iowa, $395.

Rocker with wooden design surrounded by leather on back rail; 25" arm to arm, 39" high. In Wisconsin, $295.

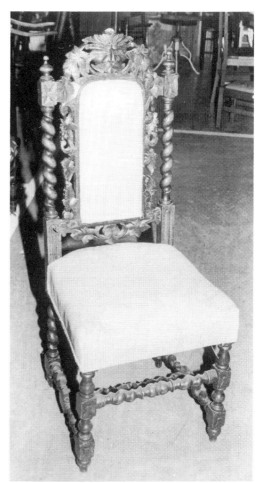

Rocker with demiarms, needlepoint seat, and brass decorations on top slat; 43" high. In Tennessee, $135.

Side chair with upholstered seat and back panel; 43" high. In Tennessee, $1,195 for a set of six.

Wooden-seat armchair with grotesque design on back rail; 25" arm to arm, 39" high. In Indiana, $325.

Captain's chair or barstool; 23" arm to arm, 30" high. In Wisconsin, $55.

Armchair; 24" arm to arm, 40" high. In Wisconsin, $95.

Captain's chair or barstool that is a 1900 copy of an early-1800s style; 20" arm to arm, 30" high. In Wisconsin, $500 for a set of four.

Cane-seat quadruple-pressed-back rocker; 38" high. In Iowa, $275.

Church or lodge chair with upholstered seat and back panel; 31" arm to arm, 26" deep, 72" high. In Indiana, $195.

Close-up of quadruple-pressed-back rocker.

*Wooden-seat double-pressed-back armchair; 25"
arm to arm, 41" high. In Wisconsin, $85.*

*Cane-seat single-pressed-back swivel chair; 24"
arm to arm, 46" high. In Iowa, $165.*

Wooden-seat swivel chair; 26" arm to arm, 34" high. In Wisconsin, $195.

Victorian side chair with upholstered seat and back; 38" high. In Illinois, $98.

5
Tables and Stands Abound

Dining tables, parlor tables and stands, and library tables.

Did You Know?

☐ The *round pedestal extension table* with extra leaves is the favored dining room table. Those with ornate carvings, however, are more costly than the plainer varieties.

☐ *Rectangular oak tables* generally are slower to sell than the round ones, according to dealers.

☐ *Refectory* or *draw tables* are rectangular tables with a double top. The lower level is divided so that it can be drawn out and pulled up at each end to add to the table's length. Many of these are English imports.

☐ The *American Windsor chair* of the 1700s is graceful, with many slender spindles in its back. *Splayed* (slanted out) legs went into the seat—that was generally scooped out to resemble a saddle. Customarily, no apron was present. The so-called *oak captain's chair* or barstool of the early 1900s is a *debased Windsor*.

☐ The *first commercial radio broadcast* was aired in 1920 in the United States. Special tables were manufactured to hold the radio and its speaker.

☐ The top of a *tilt-top table* may be in its common parallel-to-the-floor position, or it may be flipped so that the top rests perpendicular to the floor.

☐ A *tavern table* is constructed so that the top remains uncluttered for card playing. Underneath the top and usually at each corner are compartments where participants can keep their beverages or snacks.

Round extension table and four single-pressed-back chairs; 38" high, table 45" diameter, 29" high. In Iowa, $525 for a set of 4 chairs; $475 for table.

☐ *Gesso,* with a plaster of Paris base, can be carved, gilted, or painted for use as raised decorations on furniture.

How eagerly the hostesses of the 1850s must have greeted the appearance of an improved extension table. No longer was it necessary to move a series of tables (some of varying heights) together in order to entertain dinner guests.

On circular pedestal-base extension tables there were many ingenious methods used to accommodate the leaves as the table was extended. In one example, a wide, sturdy pedestal with four legs surrounding it remains stationary while the four legs pull

Round extension pedestal table with paw and ball feet and three 11" leaves; 59" wide, 48" deep with one leaf in position, 31" high. In Wisconsin, $1,995.

Round extension double-pedestal table with paw feet; 42" diameter, 29" high. In Iowa, $750.

Extension table with self-storing leaf at each end and center-support leg; 44" square, 30" high. In Wisconsin, $995.

Round extension pedestal table with claw feet; 45" diameter, 30" high. In Illinois, $695.

out to support the expanded top. In another type, the pedestal splits in half to help the legs support the load. At times, an extra leg is exposed within the pedestal and occupies a central supportive position. Yet another version features two round pillar-shaped legs that roll out on casters to hold the top securely when it is expanded. Occasionally, suspended legs are provided, which drop down for support.

Consumers usually pay less for pedestal tables with plain feet than for those with terminating features such as paw feet, claws, or claws clenching balls. Lions' heads, carved grotesques, or griffins often adorn legs.

Extension table with lion's heads and paw-feet leg structure, and four 11" leaves; 52" × 59" with two leaves in position, 29" high. In Wisconsin, $2,795.

Draw or refectory table; 30" × 42", 30" high, and 12" pull-out leaves. In Wisconsin, $495.

Dinette or breakfast set with table and two chairs from the 1930s; table 36" × 22", 31" high with two 11" drop leaves; chairs 36" high. In Iowa, $285 for the set.

Dinette or breakfast set with quarter-sawed oak drop-leaf table and two Windsor-style chairs from the 1920s; table 32" × 24", 31" high with two 11" drop leaves; chairs, 36" high. In Iowa, $300 for the set.

Back in the Middle Ages (circa 476 B.C. to 1450 A.D.), monastery dining rooms were called refectories. The long narrow tables at which monks sat down to eat were dubbed *refectory tables.* Later versions of these tables, which had stretchers close to the floor and double tops, were given the same name.

The lower level was divided so that it could be drawn out and pulled up at each end to add to the table's length. In this manner, more guests could be seated. Many such tables (also called *draw tables*) found at antiques shops and shows, are English imports.

Rectangular or oval drop-leaf tables may or may not have provisions for additional leaves. During the Depression Era of the 1920s and 1930s many small tables of this sort were listed as dinette or breakfast types. Frequently, they wore decorative decals and stenciled or free-hand designs on each corner.

Others were partially or fully painted with perhaps a band of color at the edges of the top. Muted tones such as ivory, violet, green parchment, ash gray, or seal brown gave the kitchen decors a boost. *Canted* (slanted out) legs were prevalent, and touches of color frequently highlighted their grooves or their turnings. Router lines were also accented with a line of paint.

The chairs that completed the sets were designed to match their respective tables. Those with arched tops, central splat, and turned spindles were advertised as *the beautiful cathedral style.* Sets were also provided *naked* (or without any finish) so a buyer could save money by decorating the set at home.

The 1920s and 1930s chairs that are referred to as *Windsors* have hoop backs with plain spindles and splayed legs. Beyond this point, their relationship to American Windsors of the 1700s ceases to exist.

Instead of only four spindles, the early chairs had many. The legs slanted upward toward the seat and their tops usually penetrated the surface of the saddle seat. This shape was scooped out with a higher center

Round pedestal-base table; 36" diameter, 28" high. In Illinois, $275.

Extension table with center-support leg and six leaves made by the Kiel Manufacturing Company, Manufacturers of Tables, Kiel, Wisconsin. They also made cabinets for Atwater-Kent radios. In Iowa, $895.

Extension table with center-support leg and four leaves; 45" × 30", 30" high. In Wisconsin, $400.

Extension table with one leaf; 42" square, 30" high. In Wisconsin, $195.

to comfortably accommodate the body's contours. Although the grace of the true Windsor is not present in the inexpensive kitchen or dinette chair of the 1920s and 1930s period, the general configuration exists.

"Captain's" or "bar" stools are also debased Windsors. At the other extreme, there were companies during this period that faithfully copied the early Windsors. These chairs were not parts of less-expensive dinette or breakfast sets.

Extension table with center-support leg and three leaves; 44" square, 29" high. In Wisconsin, $1,295.

Parlor table with carved relief heads on drawers and apron ends; 26" × 19", 29" high. In Illinois, $1,150.

Palette table made to resemble artist's palette; 28" wide, 24" deep, 29" high. In Michigan, $400.

Radio table that provides space for speakers on base shelf; 27" wide, 19" deep, 29" high. In Michigan, $275.

Now leave the dining room. Look around your living or recreation room. How many tables or stands do you have and what purpose do they serve? In your home, a plant may sit on one while a lamp sits on another. Do you call them tables or stands? Quite often the smaller varieties are for plants, while pedestals hold fernery or statuary, depending on the owner's preference. Larger versions are used for lamps and bric-a-brac.

There are many collectors who seek the unusual. Extremely ornate pieces please them because these pieces are not frequently seen. Pictured here is an ornate table with bas relief grotesque heads on the one drawer, apron, and feet. Scrolls and drop finials are accents, also. The table's price is high because it was expensive to buy when it was first marketed, and its decorations cause it to attract favorable attention from those who seek something different.

Tilt-top pedestal table from the 1920s with brass caps on feet; 40" diameter, 29" high. In Kentucky, $395.

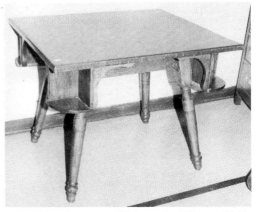

Splay-legged tavern table from the 1930s or 1940s with beverage holders at each corner; 39" wide, 33" deep, 30" high. In Wisconsin, $425.

Another table has a gentler appearance, but the palette shape of its top and base shelf distinguish it from ordinary tables. See the illustration.

The appearance of radios brought the need for a new table. After many years of experimentation by scientifically-minded men in various countries, the first commercial radio broadcast went on the air in 1920 in the United States. Phonograph records provided the music.

It was exciting to the nation when late that same year the Harding-Cox election returns, a popular newsworthy event, was reported on the air. It was necessary to wear earphones attached to the radio in order to hear the broadcast. By the mid-1920s, separate loud speakers replaced the earphones so that all in the room were able to listen. Special tables on which to place the radio, and which provided space for the speaker, were manufactured. An example of such a table is shown. The bottom shelf provided room for the speaker.

Tilt-top tables helped save space in parlors when the top was in the vertical, rather than horizontal, position. In the 1800s, these tables often functioned as servers when ladies sipped tea at social gatherings. Note the brass metal tips on the legs of the oak table, from the 1920s era.

Quarter-sawed oak pedestal table with Empire scroll feet; 24" diameter, 29" high. In Wisconsin, $185.

Although it once was not a socially acceptable table for a home, today, an oak tavern table is handy as an entertaining center. The surface is clear so that games can be played on it. Each participant has a small compartment at the corner of the table to hold drinks and snacks. The tavern table pictured is a late model from the 1930s or 1940s.

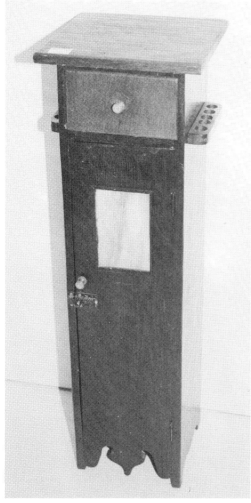

*Smoking and pipe stand with slag-door insert; 12"
square, 36" high. In Illinois, $95.*

*Quarter-sawed oak parlor table with glass balls
held by metal claw feet; 22" square, 29" high. In
Tennesee, $295.*

Some have rope-like turnings, or those similar to elongated beads or spools. Some taper
gently to become thin at the bottom.

The *cabriole leg* has a double curve that
bulges at the top, sweeps in, and then swings
out slightly once again at the foot. Feet may
be in the form of claws clutching glass balls.
They can resemble an animal's paw or they
can have metal caps. Examples can be seen
in this chapter.

While most stands share the characteristics of tables, a type that differs is the
stand designed for the smoker. The one pictured has a *slag glass* (marble-looking
opaque glass streaked with color) panel in its
door. Appendages on each side hold pipes.

Ornamentation on stands varies. For
example, *gesso* has a plaster of Paris base
that is formed into slightly raised (bas relief)
designs. It can be sculptured, carved,
molded, gilted or painted. The oak fern
stand pictured has a vase with flowers in the
front-recessed panel and a shell design on
the sides. Incised carving surrounds the
panel.

Oak tables from the early 1900s sometimes have rolled-scroll feet, similar to the
kind that were popular on the Empire furniture of the early 1800s. Catalogues from the
first of this century adopted a different name
for this style when they called it *Colonial.*

Tables can have oval, round, square,
rectangular, or shaped tops, often with scal-
lops. Their aprons come with or without
drawers and with or without base shelves.
Tops can be mounted on pedestals or on
legs.

Tables can be plain or fancy. Their legs
are straight, splayed, reeded, or bulbous.

Fern stand with applied gesso decorations in panels; 18" × 13", 37" high. In Indiana, $360.

Knick-knack table; 22" diameter, 28" high. In Michigan, $400.

Many other tables (including library tables) and stands are pictured here. Note that each has its own very special characteristics.

While many types of tables appear in this book, there are numerous others that are also worthy of photographing. If you don't see *your* cherished table, please consult the Swedberg's *American Oak Furniture Styles and Prices, Revised and Book II.* All of the illustrations are different in each of the three volumes.

And, if you still can't find your very own treasured table, remember that there were thousands of factories turning out products, each striving to catch a share of the buying public's money. Occasionally, a do-it-yourselfer crafted his own one-of-a-kind creation, perhaps to delight his wife or to present as a bridal gift. You should be pleased if your table differs from the norm.

Victorian parlor table with incised and applied decorations, drop finials at corners, and ball and stick stretchers; 31" × 22", 30" high. In Wisconsin, $235.

Lamp or plant stand with brass feet; 17" square, 30" high. In Wisconsin, $575.

Victorian oval parlor table with ash top and walnut base accented with center-support column, spindles, and applied decorations made of ash; 34" wide, 26" deep, 31" high. In Wisconsin, $395.

Quarter-sawed oak parlor table with double top, round column legs, and base shelf; 24" square, 29" high. In Michigan, $350.

Lamp or plant stand with splayed legs; 16" diameter, 29" high. In Illinois, $125.

Plant stand with splayed legs; 17" square, 30" high. In Wisconsin, $125.

Plant or lamp stand; 15" square, 30" high. In Iowa, $145.

Parlor table with splayed legs and base shelf; 24" square, 30" high. In Wisconsin, $150.

Parlor table with "turtle" top, base shelf, and paw feet; 28" wide, 23" deep, 29" high. In Wisconsin, $145.

Parlor table with octagonal scalloped top and reeded legs; 20" wide, 20" deep, 30" high. In Michigan, $150.

Standing ash-tray stand made by Stickley Bros., Grand Rapids, Michigan; 10" diameter, 30" high. In Illinois, $195.

Parlor table with ball-and-stick maple-base shelf; 24" square, 29" high. In Illinois, $125.

Library table; 36" wide, 24" deep, 28" high. In Iowa, $225.

Parlor table with splayed rope legs, ball-and-stick apron and scalloped-bottom shelf; 24" square, 30" high. In Indiana, $295.

Two smoking stands; left stand 13" square, 27" high. In Indiana, $42.50. Right stand 13" square, 29" high. In Indiana, $110.

Fern stand; 17" square, 39" high. In Indiana, $375.

Plant stand with oval top; 16" wide, 11" deep, 30" high. In Michigan, $85.

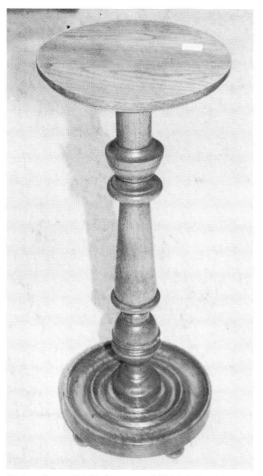

Pedestal stand; 12" diameter, 30" high. In Wisconsin, $98.50.

Pedestal; 13" diameter, 33" high. In Wisconsin, $88.

Library table with ball and stick construction on base shelf, beading on apron, and incised decorations; 36" wide, 24" deep, 31" high. In Wisconsin, $325.

Library table; 36" wide, 24" deep, 28" high. In Wisconsin, $465.

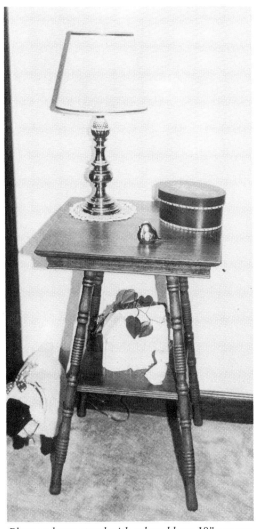

Plant or lamp stand with splayed legs; 18" square, 28" high. In Iowa, $125.

Four-shelf stand; 15" wide, 14" deep, 36" high. In Iowa, $85.

Library table; 48" wide, 29" deep, 30" high. In Iowa, $475.

Parlor table from the 1920s or 1930s; 42" wide, 24" deep, 29" high. In Iowa, $220.

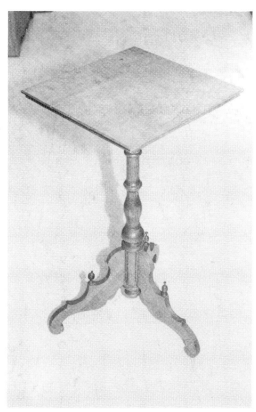

Plant stand; 11" square, 29" high. In Wisconsin, $75.

Pedestal plant stand; 15" square, 29" high. In Wisconsin, $100.

6
Bedroom Furnishings

Dressing tables, washstands, beds, dressers, chiffoniers, chifforobes, and wardrobes.

Did You Know?

☐ *Dressing* or *vanity tables and benches* became important around 1920 when many women began to use makeup. It was convenient to have a place to keep their cosmetics and to sit before a mirror while they were applied.

☐ *Washstands* were needed in homes, hotels and business establishments in the preplumbing days. These stands provided space where a wash bowl and pitcher could be kept, and where a towel could be hung.

☐ *Folding beds* were patented in the late 1800s. Some served only this single function while others had multipurpose units. Combinations often included dressers, desks, and bookcases.

☐ A *cheval mirror* is a large, swinging, looking glass mounted on a frame. It usually stands on the floor so that a viewer is able to see a full-length reflection. The *cheval dresser* received its name because it includes a tall swinging mirror that is supported in a frame.

☐ *Ash bedroom furniture* was manufactured in the last half of the 1800s. It was less expensive than similarly styled walnut pieces.

☐ *Decks* were small encased drawers mounted on the tops of dressers. Today they are generally called *handkerchief boxes*.

☐ *Boxes* fastened on the dresser top had hinged lift lids.

Vanity and chair from the 1920s; vanity 40" wide, 20" deep, 57" high; chair 30" high. In Illinois, $300.

☐ A *chiffonier* is a tall chest of drawers. Currently, many people refer to them as *highboys*.

☐ *Bombé fronts or sides* swell or bulge out. They are convex.

☐ A *chifforobe* has a chest of drawers on one side and a narrow wardrobe on the other.

□ A *wardrobe* is a piece of furniture in which clothes are hung. Some come in knock-down or break-down varieties that are pegged, and tongue and grooved so they can be taken apart readily for ease in transporting.

Does it seem possible that oak bedroom furniture can be so varied? There are dressing (*vanity*) tables with chairs or stools, washstands, chiffoniers, chifforobes, dressers, chests, wardrobes, and beds. A versatile piece was a combination secretary and wardrobe that featured a full length closet on one side and on the other, a desk space that included an upper compartment, a drop leaf for writing, and drawers beneath.

In the strict, moralistic 1800s, women might pinch their cheeks to add color or pat their noses with a bit of powder, but generally, only worldly American females used cosmetics in the days prior to World War I.

After the hostilites terminated in 1918, women experienced a new freedom. Because many of them had taken over male jobs when the men marched off to serve their country, these new wage earners achieved a degree of independence. They did not want to regress to subsidiary roles once again. Some shortened both their long tresses and their street sweeping dresses. In order to improve their appearance, ladies began to use makeup, and magazine articles encouraged this practice.

Furniture manufacturers realized that a primping place was needed—so they designed dressing tables with mirrors where cosmetics could be kept. A matching stool or chair was included so a lady could comb her hair and apply makeup in a leisurely fashion. This type of furnishing was also known, for obvious reasons, as a vanity. If such a table had a central stationary mirror and two hinged side mirrors, mademoiselle could adjust them in order to inspect her head from any angle. These dressing tables are showing a revival in popularity among the ladies today.

Before water was piped into hotels and business places, washstands were needed. Elite washstands with reservoirs were mar-

Hotel washstand with lift lid that exposes a white marble basin and drain board. Label on back reads, " The Windsor Combination Washstand, Pat. Jan. 14, 1890. The Windsor Folding Bed Co., Chicago." 31" wide, 27" deep, 58" high. In Kentucky, $1,800.

keted. Such pieces appealed to the residents of luxury hotels. A stand retrieved from the old Bault Hotel, Louisville, Kentucky had a label on its back that identifies it as: "The Windsor Combination Washstand Pat. Jan. 14, 1890."

The label includes these directions:

Directions to fill Reservoir, remove waste water jar beneath and empty same. After filling Reservoir, replace water jar which locks Reservoir, thereby preventing putting more water into tank until waste water is again emptied. Our patent device overcomes objections to similar stands by compelling removal of waste water jar before refilling reservoir, thus preventing overflow.
The Windsor Folding Bed Co., Chicago

The Windsor Combination Washstand showing the white marble basin and drain board.

Washstand commode with mirror, towel bar, and projection serpentine drawer; 33" wide, 17" deep, 65" high. In Illinois, $350.

Photographs illustrate this stand in both an open and closed position. When the lid is lifted, the faucet, top marble basin, and drain board are exposed.

Advertised as a hotel washstand, a common version required pitchers of water to be carried in so the room's occupants could wash themselves. An accompanying wash bowl was available, and a towel bar held the necessary towel. Mirrors were an added asset. A serpentine projection front juts out over the base of an illustrated hotel stand.

Washstand commode with towel bar and serpentine drawer front; 31" wide, 17" deep, 51" high. In Illinois, $235.

Bases on washstands differed. Some had one long drawer with two doors beneath. Others had three drawers and one door where necessary items could be kept. These stands were standard equipment prior to the development of inside plumbing facilities, but by the 1930s they were becoming passé.

Folding beds manufactured in the early 1900s could be just that—or they could have dual functions. A versatile version was listed in an 1897 Montgomery Ward catalogue as a combination folding bed, wardrobe, writing desk, and bookcase. Also advertised was a combination folding bed, bookcase, and writing desk. Because it is a handsome piece with elaborate carving, including a grotesque on the drop-lid writing surface, the illustrated example commands a high price even though the concealed bed portion is no longer present. Its function as a bookcase desk has not been impaired by this loss, but it would be even more desirable if it were still intact as originally manufactured.

Examine the photographs of various beds. Applied carving on the head- and footboards was commonly present. Incised designs also prevailed, and today, these decorations that have a scooped-out appearance are often referred to as *spoon carving*. Originally they were called *chip carving*. As the years pass, terminology does change.

Bedroom pieces were priced individually or as sets. Catalogues of the early 1900s frequently used the terms *washstand* and *commode* interchangeably. Shown is a suit with a washstand that matches a bed with a roll on the footboard.

A three-piece bedroom suit is highlighted in two photographs. One shows the ornate headboard and the other pictures the commode placed inside the bed's frame. The dresser is not pictured. There are deep garland carvings on both the bed and the dresser, with the latter incorporating candle or lamp stands on its mirror frame so the user's reflection can easily be seen. Further elite touches include the well-executed use of incised lines and the presence of a series of short spindles that makes the tops of the pieces distinctive.

Combination folding bed (missing), bookcase, and writing desk; 55" wide, 27" deep, 77" high. In Kentucky, $1,400.

Bed with applied decorations on head- and footboards; 57" wide, 39" high footboard, 79" high headboard. In Tennessee, $525.

Bed with spoon carving; 58" wide, 33" high foot-board, 75" high headboard. In Kentucky, $495.

Commode washstand with metal towel bar on side; 32" wide, 18" deep, 29" to top, 13" back rail. In Indiana, part of a three-piece bedroom set with the dresser not pictured, $3,850 for the set.

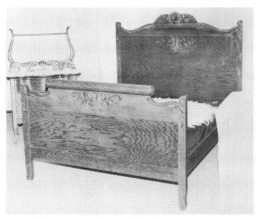

Bed and washstand commode with towel bar; bed 57" wide, 35" high footboard, 53" high headboard; commode 32" wide, 17" deep, 48" high. In Wisconsin, $775 for the set.

Headboard of bed; 76" high. In Indiana, part of a three-piece bedroom set, $3,850 for the set.

Two-piece bedroom set comprising a cheval dresser with hat box and tall cheval mirror; 45" wide, 19" deep, 81" high; and a bed 59" wide, 27" high footboard, 68" high headboard. In Illinois, $1,175 for the set.

73

Cheval dresser with hat box and tall cheval mirror; 44" wide, 21" deep, 77" high. In Indiana, $595.

A hat box that has been removed from a cheval dresser. The back rail has been added; 16" wide, 15" deep, 22" to top, 3" back rail. In Indiana, $165.

Cheval mirror; 28" wide, 78" high. In Tennessee, $325.

A cheval mirror is a large, swinging, looking glass mounted on a frame. It usually stands on the floor so that the viewer sees a full-length reflection. Also available are miniature versions that can be placed on tops of chests.

A cheval dresser receives its name because it has a tall mirror in a swinging frame. A hat cabinet and drawers provide storage space. Such a unit could be selected instead of the conventional dresser if the buyer thought it was worth the additional cost. A

A two-drawer base that was once a part of a cheval dresser; 42" wide, 19" deep, 24" high. In Iowa, $210.

Victorian ash dresser with walnut trim and fruit carved handles; 42" wide, 17" deep, 43" high. In Tennessee, $395.

Princess dresser with swing mirror and serpentine drawers; 40" wide, 21" deep, 73" high. In Iowa, $425.

two-piece bedroom set that includes a cheval dresser is illustrated.

The storage unit beside the glass on a cheval dresser is called a *hat cabinet*. Some sit flat but others have feet. A cheval dresser with the latter type compartment is shown. Often these small cabinets are removed from their original setting and are sold individually as little stands. An example of this transformation is pictured. Conversely, what a dealer calls a *lowboy* was probably the base of a cheval dresser.

Low dressers with rather large, vertically elongated swing mirrors are called *princess dressers*. They present an elegant, dainty, ladylike look. Do you suppose that's how they received their regal name? A photograph indicates that these dressers do have an attractive look.

Furniture manufactured from ash resembled that made of walnut during the Victorian era when the latter was the leading wood. The time when walnut wore the crown as King of the Woods corresponded to the years when Queen Victoria was England's longest reigning monarach (1837–1901). A photograph shows an ash dresser with *decks* (now called handkerchief boxes) on its top. The handles, oval moldings, and applied decorations are walnut. It is not unusual to find pieces that combine these two woods. This dresser was made during the last half of the 1800s.

Limbert chest of drawers with elaborately carved drawer fronts; 36" wide, 20" deep, 45" high. In Michigan, $545.

A highly carved oak chest has a "Limbert Furniture Grand Rapids & Holland, Michigan" label in the back of its top drawer. The construction with center guides, dust covers, and a spring metal on the top drawers to keep them steady as they are pulled in and out suggests that this chest is from the 1920s. The Limbert Company also made straight, plain, stoic mission furniture.

The tall, narrow chests of drawers manufactured around the turn of the century were called *chiffoniers*. Dealers and collectors currently refer to them as *highboys*, instead. They do not resemble the traditional eighteenth century form with their tall, fancy legs.

Chiffoniers, at times, have features other than their many drawers. Some have mirrors, some have compartments for gloves or other small articles, and others have both of these features. A chiffonier seen during our travels was stamped on its back with the big bold letters CHIFF.

Chiffonier with swing mirror and bombé (swelling out) front and sides; 36" wide, 19" deep, 74" high. In Illinois, $595.

Chifforobe with pull-out mirror above door and drawer section on left; 44" wide, 20" deep, 62" high. In Ohio, $500.

Notice the one in the illustration. It has the mirror, compartment, drawers, plus applied decorations, and the seldom-seen bombé sides. Because of its uniqueness, its price is correspondingly higher than the more common varieties.

A chifforobe is an article of furniture that has a chest of drawers on one side and a narrow wardrobe on the other. Some have mirrors. Occasionally, one is seen with a drop lid that serves as a writing surface. A picture of one of these is included for the reader to examine.

Dealers speak of knock-down or breakdown wardrobes. Most large wardrobes are heavy to move about. They're too bulky to haul in small trucks, and they don't like to go up curving staircases, around bends, down narrow halls, or through doorways. Because of this, some ingenious person constructed a wardrobe that could easily be taken apart and reassembled as desired.

Usually, no tools are required—pegs, slots, and tongue-and-groove construction afford an easy take-apart/put-together design. The resulting product is sturdy and secure. If you disassemble such a wardrobe, it may prove helpful to mark the pieces where they fit together for ease in reassembling.

A couple (who will not be mentioned by name because it would be too embarassing) had a heavy wardrobe they struggled to move about. They lifted the feet onto rugs and tugged and pushed it from room to room on many occasions. Finally, after years of ownership, they learned the wardrobe was a knock-down type. Wouldn't you think that writers of books about furniture would know better?

Pictured is a ceiling scrapping wardrobe that, fortunately, breaks down into ten pieces. In days of yore, people hung their garments on hooks or pegs on the wall since they didn't have closets. When factories produced wardrobes, clothes were hung in

Breakdown wardrobe with ornate cornice and two drawers at base; 48" wide, 17" deep, 94" high. In Illinois, $1,250.

Ash commode washstand with towel bar that is not original; 30" wide, 18" deep, 59" high. In Illinois, $200.

Commode washstand with beveled mirror, brass towel bar and candle or lamp shelves; 36" wide, 18" deep, 70" high. In Wisconsin, $625.

them, a much better way to keep garments free from dust, buzzing flies, and other dirt-producing elements.

Wardrobes can have a single or double door, and some have mirrors on their door sections.

Did you ever realize how many styles of oak furniture are available for use in a bedroom? This wide selection affords the oak advocates a great deal of individuality in decorating their homes.

Oak and ash bureau washstand; 32" wide, 18" deep, 30" high, 4" back rail, splashback or "splasher" as it was called in early catalogues. In Wisconsin, $185.

Commode washstand with towel bar and serpentine drawer front; 33" wide, 18" deep, 60" high. In Wisconsin, $250.

Dresser with swing mirror, applied decorations and serpentine top drawers; 36" wide, 20" deep, 63" high. In Wisconsin, $325.

Bed with roll tops on foot and headboard, and scroll feet; 55" wide, 41" high footboard, 47" high headboard. In Illinois, $235.

Bed with applied decorations; 57" wide, 74" high. In Illinois, $495.

Elm and ash commode washstand with towel bar and serpentine drawer front; 34" wide, 19" deep, 53" high. In Iowa, $275.

Ash dresser with swing mirror, applied decorations and serpentine front; 43" wide, 20" deep, 73" high. In Wisconsin, $265.

Ash bed with incised designs and applied decorations; 57" wide, 72" high. In Indiana, part of a three-piece bedroom set with commode and dresser (not pictured), $1,095 for the set.

Bed with applied decorations; 58" wide, 35" high footboard, 79" high headboard. In Wisconsin, part of a two-piece bedroom set with the dresser not pictured, $1,295 for the set.

Dresser with swing mirror, applied decorations, and serpentine front; 50" wide, 23" deep, 72" high. In Wisconsin, $295.

Dresser with swing mirror and applied decorations; 45" wide, 22" deep, 77" high. In Wisconsin, $375.

Bed with applied decorations; 59" wide, 34" high footboard, 73" high headboard. In Iowa, $395.

Child's toy dresser; 21" wide, 10" deep, 19" high, 3" rail. In Wisconsin, $120.

Chest of drawers; 50" wide, 24" deep, 51" high. In Kentucky, $350.

Night stand with cabriole leg and serpentine front; 22" wide, 16" deep, 30" high. In Iowa, $245.

Chiffonier with applied decorations on drawers and vertical beading on stiles; 33" wide, 20" deep, 50" high. In Indiana, $525.

Chiffonier with applied decorations on back rail and hat box; 33" wide, 19" deep, 45" high, 8" rail. In Iowa, $325.

Dresser with swing mirror and applied decorations; 43" wide, 19" deep, 74" high. In Illinois, $285.

Dresser with swing mirror and applied decorations; 42" wide, 19" deep, 77" high. In Wisconsin, $295.

Victorian dresser with applied decorations and projection top drawer; 40" wide, 19" deep, 42" high. In Wisconsin, $395.

Blanket chest with carved decoration on front and large copper hinges; 35" wide, 18" deep, 18" high. In Michigan, $450.

Chiffonier with swing mirror and projection top drawer; 33" wide, 21" deep, 72" high. In Iowa, $495.

Combination wardrobe and desk with full length beveled mirror on wardrobe door, and desk with mirror and fall front; 52" wide, 13" deep, 77" high. In Kentucky, $1,250.

Chiffonier with swing mirror, hat box compartment and serpentine front; 34" wide, 21" deep, 73" high. In Wisconsin, $1,450.

Chiffonier; 40" wide, 21" deep, 46" high, 3" rail. In Wisconsin, $575.

Larkin chiffonier with serpentine top drawers and original label on the back; 34" wide, 19" deep, 51" high, 5" rail. In Iowa, $345.

Larkin chiffonier with original label on the back; 34" wide, 17" deep, 46" high, 4" rail. In Iowa, $265.

Chifforobe with a pull-out shelf between the two top drawers; 41" wide, 19" deep, 60" high. In Wisconsin, $325.

Chifforobe with full length beveled mirror on door and beveled swing mirror above the drawers; 44" wide, 20" deep, 67" high. In Kentucky, $265.

Ash Victorian dresser with two decks or "hankie" boxes, applied carving on drawers and mirror frame, and candle or lamp shelves on mirror frame; 41" wide, 21" deep, 72" high. In Wisconsin, $695.

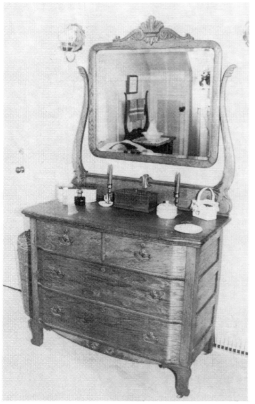

Dresser with swing mirror and applied decorations; 42" wide, 22" deep, 74" high. In Iowa, $285.

Chiffonier with swing mirror and serpentine front; 33" wide, 18" deep, 72" high. In Ohio, $345.

Wardrobe with one drawer and one door; 32" wide, 17" deep, 82" high. In Illinois, $525.

Wardrobe with one door; 28" wide, 24" deep, 72" high. In Wisconsin, $495.

Wardrobe with applied decorations, serpentine base and drawer, and paw feet; 44" wide, 22" deep at base, 85" high. In Iowa, $1,395.

Ash Eastlake dresser with two decks or "hankie" boxes, incised designs, burl walnut panels on drawers, swing mirror, and candle or lamp shelves on mirror frame. Made in Lansing, Michigan; 39" wide, 18" deep, 80" high. In Michigan, $800.

Wardrobe with two drawers and two doors; 40" wide, 15", deep 79" high. In Indiana, $595.

Chiffonier with swing mirror; 28" wide, 19" deep, 71" high. In Wisconsin, $325.

7
Storage Units

Sideboards, buffets, china cabinets, kitchen cabinets, wall cabinets, cupboards, and iceboxes.

Did You *Know?*

□ A *buffet,* according to Webster's definition, is a piece of furniture with drawers and cupboards for dishes, table linens, silver, etc.—a *sideboard.* We, then, will use two terms—*buffet* and *sideboard*—interchangeably.

□ *Supporting columns* on furniture can have either a masculine or feminine motif. A *caryatid* is a female figure that serves in this capacity. An *atlantes,* on the other hand, is a male image that also functions as a supporting column.

□ A *pilaster* is an artificial decorative pillar with no structural strength, that is set against a background. Frequently, it is half round or rectangular.

□ A *china buffet* is a cross between a sideboard and a china cabinet, embodying characteristics of each.

□ *China cabinets,* because of their popularity, are currently being reproduced.

□ *Minerva* was a Roman goddess of wisdom and war, but surprisingly, she was also the goddess of necessary household arts and crafts—such as spinning and weaving. Artists often depicted her wearing a war helmet.

□ A *baker's cabinet* evolved from a table that had such features as a bin for flour, pull-out boards for kneading and cutting, perhaps a divided bin for meal and sugar, drawers for cutlery and linen, and provisions for pans.

Quarter-sawed oak sideboard or buffet with grotesques on stiles and caryatid columns supporting the top shelf; 54" wide, 24" deep, 67" high. In Indiana, $595.

□ *Hoosier cabinets* were manufactured in New Castle, Indiana. Many other factories produced a similar type, but *Hoosier* became the generic name for all similar examples.

□ The *time payment plan* was becoming established in the 1920s. The challenge to buy now, pay easy installments later, helped attract customers.

□ A *tambour* is defined as both a slatted, flexible shutter that can be opened sideways or vertically, and as a flexible door that operates in grooves and is made of thin strips of wood glued to a duck or linen backing.

□ A *pie safe* with punched tin panels or screens was a storage unit for baked goods. It allowed air circulation and kept pesty rodents and flies away from the food.

□ *Cupboards* presently have different, descriptive titles. A closed or blind one has solid wooden doors. An open cupboard may have doors with glass panes or may have no doors at all. A *step-back* has a top that sits slightly back on its base and is smaller in depth than its base. A *straight-front* cupboard has a continuous straight-up-and-down line.

□ *Iceboxes* were referred to as *refrigerators* in old catalogues. Because they are in great demand, they are currently being made.

Built-in cupboards were not extensively used in the late 1800s and early 1900s. Therefore, in order for the old adage *a place for everything and everything in its place* to be obeyed, furniture in dining rooms and kitchens had to include storage facilities.

Buffets or sideboards with their drawers and cupboard spaces were either plain or they were well endowed with decorative features. In differentiating between the two, dealers tend to apply the term *buffet* to the humbler, less ostentatious versions, and reserve the title *sideboard* for the larger, more ornamental structure. This distinction, however, is not used in this chapter.

On sideboards with generous proportions, supporting columns were frequently carved to represent the human male or female figure. The female is a *caryatid* while the male is called an *atlantes*. Two caryatids perform their supportive duty of holding up a shelf on the mirrored top of the quarter-sawed buffet that's pictured. The base has turned *pilasters* (nonfunctional, decorative pillars) with grotesques at their apex.

China buffet with scrolled Empire feet and shelf supports and beveled mirror; 44" wide, 20" deep, 54" high; Seth Thomas mantel clock with artificial oak graining. In Wisconsin, buffet $525, clock $225.

China buffet with two glass china closets flanking an enclosed central storage area and a secret drawer at the base of the left side; 48" wide, 15" deep, 62" high. In Illinois, $885.

China cabinet with round columns and paw feet, and three panels of convex glass; 36" wide, 13" deep, 63" high. In Wisconsin, $695.

China cabinet with three panels of convex glass, leaded glass at the top of center door, applied decorations, and paw feet; 43" wide, 15" deep, 69" high. In Illinois, $1,550.

Since a china buffet is a cross between a china cabinet and a buffet, it inherits features from both of them. Generally, there's a plush-lined drawer for silverware and a space reserved for tablecoths and napkins. Instead of a storage compartment with solid wooden doors, a glass covered area exposes to view an array of daintily designed dishes or glittering glass objects that comprise the family's table settings. This display section may be either on the front or on the sides. A picture of each is shown.

A china cabinet was a delight to a housewife who enjoyed the dainty wares available in the early 1900s. It offered a sanctuary where her delicate treasures were arranged neatly for all to see. China with sentimental meaning to its owner included dishes imported as *blanks* that represented well known back stamps from many European countries. These blanks were hand-painted by women who followed the prevailing trend of attending china decorating classes. They added the colorful roses or fruit and often signed their works. These became personalized gifts on birthdays and wedding days. There were clubs where members received colorful cups and saucers on birthdays and wedding anniversaries.

For china cabinets that did not have straight sides, a catalogue description read *swell shaped glass* to describe the sides or the doors that bulged out. Today the term *convex* succinctly describes this characteristic.

Corner china cabinets are not as evident as are the more numerous flat-backs. It is sometimes difficult, in a modern house, to find an appropriate spot that's free from electrical outlets, heating ducts, windows, or other encumbrances where such a closet can be placed.

Corner china cabinet with two doors, beveled shield mirror near top, and Minerva-type carved head at the apex; 42" wide, 17" deep, 75" high. In Indiana, $1,995.

Dry sink cabinet with pull out dough board supported by attached leg; 52" wide, 30" deep, 70" high. In Indiana, $1,175.

Kitchen cabinet, called by various names including "Baker's Cabinet," "Doughboy Cupboard" and "Possum Belly"; 43" wide, 27" deep, 71" high. In Indiana, $575.

An ornament on one corner cabinet is the carved head of a woman wearing a warrior's protective helmet. This is Minerva, who was the goddess of wisdom and war. The household arts of spinning and weaving were her domain also, but artists like to picture her in her war attire. She appeared more frequently on the skillfully executed furniture in the Victorian walnut era than she did on the turn-of-the-century oak and its look-alikes.

Today's prepared food mixes and instant preparations were not available in the early 1900s. Then, it was the common practice to start from scratch when preparing meals. In kitchens, cabinets and cupboards with work areas were handy essentials.

Two-piece Hawkeye kitchen cabinet made by the Union Furniture Co., Burlington, Iowa; 47" wide, 28" deep, 81" high. In Illinois, $1,150.

Hoosier kitchen cabinet with tambour sliding doors and porcelain pull-out work area; 41" wide, 26" deep as seen, 71" high. In Indiana, $595.

One unusual kitchen cabinet includes a dry sink where a housewife worked as she prepared the family's food or where she tidied up after meals. Since rural residents with hungry farm hands and family members to feed tended to have homemade bread and pies, this cabinet incorporated a pull-out area with its own supporting leg. This area provided a surface on which to work the dough. Additional helpful features were the flour bin and cutting board.

Baker's cabinet is the presently used term for a table that incorporates a bin for flour, pull-out boards for kneading and cutting, a sometimes-present divided bin shared by meal on one side and sugar on the other, drawers for cutlery and linen, and provisions for pans. As much as 50 pounds of flour or sugar were kept in one of those bins.

To utilize space well, it seemed practical to put a cupboard top on the table to provide additional storage. A dealer calls cabinets with these features *doughboys*. Old catalogues simply refer to them as kitchen cabinets.

Hoosier cabinets were made in New Castle, Indiana. Since Indiana is known as the Hoosier State, it is fitting that the manufacturer associated this name with its product. What is not known for certain is how this moniker originated. If the traditional pioneer greeting of visitors, "who's here," is slurred slightly, it sounds like the name. Another version says *husher* was a slang title for a fighting man who hushed opponents with his fists. At any rate, Hoosier Cabinet has become the generic name for kitchen storage units manufactured by numerous factories.

Medicine cabinet with beveled mirror and applied decorations; 18" wide, 6" deep, 24" high. In Indiana, $275.

Hoosier kitchen cabinet with label on the back that reads, "Hoosier Manufacturing Co. 'The Hoosier Kitchen Cabinets,' Newcastle, Indiana, U.S.A."; 40" wide, 28" deep, 70" high. In Indiana, $795.

Sears Roebuck and Company secured its Wilson Kitchen Cabinets from a quality factory in Grand Rapids, Michigan and boasted that it "does for the woman and her kitchen what modern machinery and labor saving devices do for the breadwinner of the family." After all, "System in the office, the store, and the factory is a very valuable asset." It is likewise essential in a kitchen, so saving steps by having necessities confined to one work area increases a homemaker's efficiency.

The Sellers Company of Elwood, Indiana, promoted a "June Bride" model and the *"Kitchen Maid."* Some other Indiana makers were Ingram Richardson Manufacturing Company of Frankfort, and Wasmuth Endicott Company of Andrews. Boone and Greencastle cabinets were also Indiana made. In neighboring Kentucky, Scheirich of Louisville produced *Hoosier* cabinets.

Found on some Hoosiers was a flexible door or *tambour* that operated in grooves. It was made of thin strips of wood glued to a duck or linen backing, and could be opened horizontally or vertically.

The time payment plan, established in the 1920s, urged people to buy now and pay later. It was possible to own a Hoosier in this way.

A gentleman who formerly was an employee at the New Castle Hoosier Cabinet factory identified one Hoosier as an early example. He further stated that the market ceased for this product in the 1940s when built-in features became standard in homes.

Another cabinet that could be in a kitchen was a medicine cabinet, but its use was not limited to storing linaments, lotions, and pills. A man's razor, shaving brush, and shaving soap were kept inside. Nearby, hung his strap for sharpening his razor blade.

Medicine cabinet with drop-lid mirrored door; 13" wide, 6" deep, 22" high. In Iowa, $105.

Oak and poplar pie safe with glass panes that have replaced the original tin panels; 43" wide, 15" deep, 54" high. In Illinois, $365.

Single-door cupboard with paneled sides, ornate cornice, and back that is also finished; 28" wide, 15" deep, 85" high. In Michigan, $1,200.

In the days when a housewife baked many pies at one time, she placed them in a pie safe. These customarily had doors with attractive punched tin designs that kept out buzzing flies and mice. Some safes merely had protective screens. The holes on each type permitted air to circulate to retard molding.

Step-back cupboard with applied decorations on cornice; 47" wide, 24" deep at base, 85" high. In Wisconsin, $950.

Straight-front cupboard with incised, spoon-carved, and applied decorations; 28" wide, 14" deep, 78" high. In Wisconsin, $1,295.

In the winter, Northern housewives, at times, stored their baked pies in the cold, unheated attic area where they froze and were preserved for later consumption.

A pie safe in which the punched tin has been replaced by panes of glass is shown. It was made from a combination of poplar and oak. Oak pie safes are not common. Most were made of pine, poplar, and walnut, and date to the last half of the 1800s.

The general public uses the name *icebox* for an insulated wooden cabinet where ice kept food and beverages cold. In contrast to this, a 1908 Sears, Roebuck & Co. catalogue pictures and labels these units as refrigerators.

*Icebox*es come in four basic sizes to accommodate 25, 50, 75, or 100 pounds of ice. In these refrigerators, air circulated continually. Based on the principle that hot air

rises, the ice section was at the top. When warm air hit the block of ice, it cooled and descended to the bottom. As it warmed, it rose again, and the cycle kept repeating itself.

The large crystal cube was inserted either through a lift-lid at the top of the cabinet or through a door that opened at the front. The former was called a top-loading ice compartment and the latter was named a front-loading ice compartment. As melting occurred, the water flowed through a tube, out a hole, into a drainage pan—which had to be emptied with regularity.

Ice was delivered to town and city customers. As late as the 1930s, a horse and wagon was used to deliver ice to customers who displayed cards in their windows. These cards indicated the amount of ice they wished to order. If the number 25 was the

Corner cupboard; 51" wide, 18" deep, 85" high. In Illinois, $1,300.

Two-piece open step-back cupboard with pie shelf and work area between the two parts; 46" wide, 26" deep, 71" high. In Wisconsin, $750.

top number on the card, that amount was delivered. The cards could be turned so that any of the other three numbers—50, 75, or 100—could be the top number.

The driver, called an ice man, picked up a precut block with ice tongs, swung it upon his leather-protected shoulder, and carried it into the house to deposit in the icebox. On hot summer days, this man was popular with the neighborhood kids who retrieved small slivers of ice from the wagon's floor. The ice was cooling to suck on and it was a challenge to see who could grab the largest piece.

During the winter, rural men and boys cooperated to obtain their ice supplies by gathering together to saw marked-off blocks from frozen rivers. These, they hauled away to a storage place—perhaps a vacant old house—where they insulated the layers with

Ash icebox with metal label reading, "The New Iceberg, Sheboygan, Wis."; 23" wide, 17" deep, 42" high. In Indiana, $420.

Double-door icebox with metal label reading, "North Pole"; 25" wide, 19" deep, 55" high. In Wisconsin, $485.

Buffet with applied decorations, reeded pillars supporting top shelf, and serpentine top drawers; 42" wide, 21" deep, 76" high. In Iowa, $540.

a thick covering of sand or sawdust. Farmers picked up ice blocks from this communal supply whenever they needed any. No tally was kept of the amount each family used.

It is interesting to find names on the small metal plaques affixed to iceboxes. *New Iceberg, Sheboygan, Wis.* is on a lift-top type. One with a front door at the top, through which blocks of ice were inserted, wears a tag that reads *North Pole*. Another name on a pictured icebox is *Victor, Challenge Refrigerator, Grand Haven, Mich., U.S.A.*

Storage units from dining rooms and kitchens of the past are being sought by families who enjoy old articles or by those who like to feature a country decor. It's quite a promotion for these cupboards and cabinets. They were disclaimed for years and demoted to garages, basements, or attics for holding miscellaneous articles before they became popular once again and rejoined the furniture of the home.

Today, these cupboards serve well in almost any room in the house. They're great for storing bulky games in a recreation area. They're greeted with enthusiasm in casual bedrooms because guys and gals can stack their slacks, jeans, and sweaters on the shelves—it's easy to keep colors separated so that only a quick glance is necessary for the owner to make a selection and extract the precise garments desired. There's no more shuffling through drawers to find what you need because everything is right there, neatly on display and within reach. That's a great way for a sleepyhead to pick out clothes to don in a hurry.

It's fun to find new uses for heritage furniture.

Buffet with applied decorations, round upper-shelf support columns, serpentine drawers, and paw feet; 48" wide, 22" deep, 78" high. In Kentucky, $650.

Buffet with applied decorations, grotesque upper-shelf support columns, three mirrors, and serpentine drawers; 48" wide, 23" deep, 85" high. In Indiana, $800.

China buffet with leaded glass doors, serpentine upper drawers, swell lower drawer, and beveled mirror; 45" wide, 21" deep, 56" high. In Wisconsin, $1,275.

Buffet with applied decorations, pressed-carved designs on door panels and mirror crest, beveled mirror, and cabriole legs; 48" wide, 18" deep, 58" high. In Iowa, $495.

Buffet with applied decorations and round columns with hoofed-type feet supporting the upper shelf; 48" wide, 22" deep, 76" high. In Iowa, $795.

Buffet with swell top drawers, beveled mirror, and paw feet; 46" wide, 21" deep, 55" high. In Iowa, $275.

Quarter-sawed oak server with bottom shelf; 42" wide, 21" deep, 42" high. In Tennessee, $395.

Server with bottom shelf; 41" wide, 18" deep, 40" high. In Wisconsin, $250.

Ash two-piece late-1800s Victorian buffet with bird's-eye maple veneer on drawers, door, and back panels; 43" wide, 20" deep, 69" high. In Illinois, $525.

China cabinet with convex glass in side panels and in central door, and mirrors in back of the two top shelves; 39" wide, 16" deep, 70" high. In Kentucky, $975.

China cabinet with convex glass in side panels, beveled mirror in the upper section of the inside, and paw feet; 50" wide, 15" deep, 63" high. In Indiana, $675.

Buffet with applied decorations, swell top drawers and brass pulls, escutcheons and hinges; 50" wide, 24" deep, 74" high. In Indiana, $995.

China cabinet with convex glass in side panels, incised carving on back rail, and spade feet; 38" wide, 14" deep, 68" high. In Iowa, $695.

China cabinet with glass shelves; 36" wide, 12" deep, 49" high. In Kentucky, $435.

Cabinet from the 1930s; 38" wide, 15" deep, 52" high. In Kentucky, $295.

China cabinet with fumed oak finish and flat glass panels in sides and door; 37" wide, 13" deep, 69" high. In Illinois, $485.

Kitchen cabinet with metal plaque reading, "Wilson Kitchen Cabinet, The Best"; 42" wide, 27" deep, 71" high. In Iowa, $475.

Hoosier kitchen cabinet, dated 1910, with copperplated original hardware and replaced porcelain knobs; 40" wide, 28" deep as seen, 68" high. In Iowa, $495.

Hoosier kitchen cabinet, dated 1931, with pulldown tambour and metal plaque reading, "Hoosier, New Castle, Indiana"; 40" wide, 24" deep, 70" high. In Illinois, $450.

Kitchen cabinet with galvanized work area; 48" wide, 26" deep, 79" high. In Illinois, $795.

Open cupboard with pie shelf; 43" wide, 26" deep, 74" high. In Wisconsin, $675.

Kitchen cabinet from the 1930s with a metal plaque reading, "Scheirich, Louisville, Ky." and with the tambour pull-down door missing; 40" wide, 26" deep, 71" high. In Kentucky, $300.

Kitchen cabinet with porcelain work surface, pull-down tambour door, and door pulls marked with an S to indicate it is a Sellers cabinet; 41" wide, 27" deep, 67" high. In Iowa, $495.

Kitchen cabinet patented March 14, 1916 with frosted glass panels in upper doors, tambour sliding doors, and original glasses and sugar container; 40" wide, 28" deep, 70" high. In Wisconsin, $795.

Kitchen cabinet with porcelain work surface, slag glass in top panels of upper doors and with a metal plaque reading, "Sellers, Elwood, Indiana"; 41" wide, 27" deep, 70" high. In Illinois, $500.

Kitchen cabinet marked "Wilson" on a metal plaque with slag glass in top panels of upper doors; the tambour pull-down door is missing; 40" wide, 25" deep, 69" high. In Illinois, $225.

Icebox marked Iceberg *on a metal plaque; 23" wide, 16" deep, 42" high. In Wisconsin, $425.*

Icebox marked with a metal plaque, "Victor, Challenge Refrigerator Co., Grand Haven, Mich. U.S.A."; 22" wide, 15" deep, 40" high. In Iowa, $400.

Icebox with porcelain lining and a metal plaque reading, "North Pole"; 38" wide, 22" deep, 56" high. In Indiana, $1,095.

Music cabinet with mirror in back rail; 19" wide, 14" deep, 37" high, 9" rail. In Wisconsin, $145.

Step-back cupboard; 39" wide, 20" deep at the base, 82" high. In Indiana, $795.

China buffet with leaded glass and carved designs; 48" wide, 18" deep, 43" high. In Iowa, $345.

Step-back cupboard; 40" wide, 19" deep, 74" high. In Illinois, $575.

Straight-front cupboard; 37" wide, 16" deep, 77" high. In Illinois, $550.

Music cabinet; 18" wide, 14" deep, 41" high. In Illinois, $115.

Straight-front cupboard; 38" wide, 16" deep, 72" high. In Illinois, $495.

8
Student Aids

Files, bookcases, and desks.

Did You Know

□ *Files* with a series of small card-size drawers are being acquired by music lovers who like to keep their cassettes and VCR tapes easily available.

□ *Larkin Soap Company* of Buffalo, New York developed a club system whereby members earned points to secure premiums that could be used to buy furniture.

□ A *bookcase-desk* listed in catalogues of the late 1800s through the 1920 era unites the two pieces side by side. Today these combination units are often referred to as *secretaries* or *side-by-sides*. Almost always the desk is on the right, but there are some for left-handed people with the desk on the left.

□ *Sectional bookcases* abounded in the early 1900s. Each glass-enclosed unit could be purchased separately and fit into place, one above the other. Bases and tops were available to complete these stack cases.

□ A *small parlor desk* was referred to by other names. It was often called a *fancy desk* or a *lady's desk*.

□ A *roll top* is a panel made of narrow, parallel, wooden slats glued to a flexible base of duck or linen.

□ A *roll-top desk* with an *S-curve* outsells its *C-curved* counterpart, according to dealers.

□ A *cylinder* is a quarter-round continuous-piece hood that moves up and down in grooves on a cylinder desk.

□ A *secretary* is a desk—usually with a bookcase above, and a series of drawers below the writing surface.

Fifty-four-drawer file cabinet made by W. C. Heller & Co., Montpelier, Ohio; 26" wide, 12" deep, 43" high. In Wisconsin, $480.

□ *Drop lid, drop front, fall front,* or *slant front* are terms used to describe a desk with a hinged lid that drops down to form a writing surface.

□ *Files, bookcases,* and *desks* are three pieces of furniture that students seek. They are also relevant parts of a business office or a home study area. It's not uncommon for a doctor, lawyer, contractor, or other professional person to achieve a unique decor

Larkin sectional bookcase with instructions that include assembly techniques; 34" wide, 12" deep, 44" high. In Iowa, $300.

through the acquisition of antiques or collectibles. To these people, the old woods add a warmth and character that plastics and metal lack.

Students in college towns like to buy floor standing files—not to hold their 3 × 5 research index cards, but to use as music centers where they keep their cassettes and VCR tapes organized and readily available.

Young people are imaginative. One lad selected two oak hymnal racks—retrieved from an old church pew—for storing his tapes, and a coed purchased a gum rack from a store display for her sonic center. The cost outlay was minimal for these two purchases when compared with the price of a file.

With the current stress on arts and crafts as home projects that can double as moneymakers for the more gifted workers, files keep spools of thread, yarn, scraps of felt, spangles, beads, quilt pieces, buttons, tape, thimbles, or whatever is within easy, seeable reach. It's amazing how much those drawers can hold.

Four-drawer file cabinet; 15" wide, 24" deep, 51" high. In Iowa, $350.

Larger, folder-size file boxes keep tabs on specialized collections or hold important papers in a neat order, as was their original purpose. A married couple, both realtors, share an office that is located in a quaint house. Through the use of antiques, the house has been transformed with care and charm into an old-time center. Their file cabinets, desks, conference tables, and chairs are all treasures from the past—yet comfortably usable today.

Now, consider *library cases,* as they were called. Around the 1920s, sectional bookcases were versatile. The separate units could be stacked one above the other, as desired, so that a buyer could build his own with the various heights available. (An early advertisement announced that sectional

Viking sectional bookcase made by Skandia Furniture Co., Rockford, Ill., patented 1908; 34" wide, 13" deep, 57" high. In Wisconsin, $425.

Bookcase; 40" wide, 13" deep, 45" high. In Tennessee, $475.

Macey sectional bookcase with bottom drawer and claw feet; 34" wide, 11" deep, 69" high. In Iowa, $600.

bookcases *grew* with your library.) The book portion came with inside measurements of 9, 11, or 13 inches, in order to accommodate both the tall and short volumes.

The glass doors pull up and slide back when the case is in an open position. They're pulled out and put down to close the case. If someone wanted to pay extra, sections with leaded glass were available.

The top and base were additional unit parts. The base could sit flush on the floor, or have claw-and-ball feet, or the scrolled Empire type. A drawer was occasionally present. One line marketed by Montgomery Ward was marked *Macey*.

Combination double bookcase-desk with convex glass doors, swell drawer beneath drop lid, and pressed decorations; 54" wide, 13" deep, 74" high. In Indiana, $1,325.

Combination bookcase-desk with convex glass door, beveled-glass mirror, applied decorations, swell drawer beneath drop lid, and paw feet; 38" wide, 12" deep, 69" high. In Iowa, $995.

The Larkin Soap Company of Buffalo, New York had an enthusiastic approach toward advertising. A club system was developed and members could accrue specified premium points by buying certain soap products. By collecting these premiums, members could save until certain prizes—including furniture—could be acquired. It was possible to accumulate enough points to secure desired awards or to use a combination of cash and coupons.

The recipient frequently had to assemble furniture that was shipped to his home. Instructions, bearing the Larkin name, for both the assembly and care of the furniture,

Combination bookcase-desk with beveled mirror and pressed designs; 36" wide, 10" deep, 70" high. In Wisconsin, $795.

Combination bookcase-desk with applied decorations, leaded glass on top panel, and fretwork designs; 39" wide, 12" deep, 71" high. In Indiana, $580.

Combination bookcase-desk; 45" wide, 13" deep, 68" high. In Iowa, $625.

were pasted on the back. Because bits of history are associated with labels on furniture, the wise person preserves them in some way. Clear vinyl, for example, can be used to cover them.

Various examples of the sectional bookcases are illustrated, with one example shown having a Larkin label.

Combination bookcase-desks were generally manufactured to accommodate the right-handed person. Not too many left-handed versions were available. During extensive traveling to make the photographs for this book, only one left-handed version was sighted. It was at Louisville's largest antique mall, but was in a difficult area to get a good shot, so a "we'll get one later on" spirit was adopted. This proved to be a mistake as we saw no others. If you're a Missouri "Show

me" resident, look on page 107 in Swedberg's *American Oak Furniture Styles and Prices, Book II* and you'll find one in the upper left-hand corner.

A left-handed combination bookcase-desk has the desk portion on the left side. The user can write with his left hand and reach with his right to secure books from the shelves. Conversely, the right-hander's desk is to the right, and the bookcase is on the other side. The matter is easy to resolve when the desk occupies a central postion flanked by a library case on each side. The result is an ambidextrous piece of furniture. Photographs of the latter two combination bookcase-desks are shown. Both have a series of drawers, and the top one in each case swells and projects over the other two.

It's interesting to note that the glass in bookcase doors can be either convex (swell front) or straight. Legs differ from the

Fall-front desk with concave top drawers, beading, and applied decorations; 29" wide, 18" deep, 44" high. In Iowa, $325.

Fall-front parlor desk with applied decorations and oval beveled mirror; 30" wide, 15" deep, 55" high. In Illinois, $495.

French *S* curve, to paws, to plain types. Mirrors, rails, shelves, and decorations are varied.

A series of drawers is not always present beneath the fall front. Instead, a door may be included. Types with open, no-door bookcases under the drop lid could be purchased. If a rod was provided, the housewife could stretch a drape that coordinated with the colors of the room, across the space.

A petite parlor desk many be referred to as a *fancy-type* or a *lady's desk*. Generally, a drop-lid section with one drawer beneath is supported by long legs, many of which have a French double-curve style.

Such fall-front parlor desks are available with drawers, or with a combination of drawers and one or two doors that provide

Fall-front parlor desk with applied decorations; 32" wide, 17" deep at base, 55" high. In Wisconsin, $495.

Fall-front desk with beveled mirrors, applied decorations, grotesque heads above shelf supports, swell drawers, and storage comaprtment with glass doors; 31" wide, 15" deep, 63" high. In Illinois, $850.

This fall-front desk, identical to the one on the left, demonstrates how prices vary in different locales. In Wisconsin, $995.

cupboard space. Each seems to have its own gallery style, incorporating such features as mirrors, beading, applied and carved decorations, or a combination of these features.

Parlor desks, at times, had glass doors under their drop lids where books could be stored. Fretwork designs might be added to enhance their appearance. Sometimes a drawer was included near the base. The stubby legs could be plain or fancy.

A small secretary-type fall-front desk resulted when a bookcase area was placed above the drop-lid section.

Sometimes a slant-lid desk did not drop down to form a writing surface. Instead the lid itself, as is, provided the writer's work area. If some article—say, a forgotten pen or a necessary note—was needed, the sloping surface had to be cleared and the lid, which was hinged at the back, had to be lifted to get the item from the storage space within.

An illustrated plantation desk from the last half of the 1800s has this characteristic. Its tall, closed-cupboard top has pigeon holes and drawers inside. The bird's-eye maple veneering on the door panels offers a contrast to the oak look-alike woods in the desk. Can you distinguish the designs in the door panels that reminded someone of a bird's eye? This decorative, distorted pattern is discovered only after the maple tree is cut.

Squared legs, often referred to as *New York legs,* were easier to fashion than those that required the work of a lathe to produce their sometimes intricate turnings. Table desks with a fall-front compartment on top, dating from approximately 1850 to 1870, had this leg style.

Plantation-type desk with bird's-eye maple door panels; 36" wide, 27" deep, 72" high. In Kentucky, $750.

Quarter-sawed oak fall-front desk with bookcase at top; 35" wide, 13" deep, 63" high. In Iowa, $945.

Larkin sewing desk with folding legs and top; 48" wide, 24" deep, 26" high. In Iowa, $235.

Table-top desk with fall-front and New York legs, circa 1870; 36" wide, 24" deep, 55" high. In Kentucky, $525.

S-curve roll-top desk patented April 30, 1907; 60" wide, 32" deep, 48" high. In Illinois, $1,350.

Quarter-sawed oak fall-front secretary with serpentine drawers and short cabriole legs; 36" wide, 18" deep, 77" high. In Tennessee $1,600.

Cylinder desk with incised decorations; 32" wide, 22" deep, 49" high. In Wisconsin, $1,195.

Labels found on articles of furniture can provide helpful information to collectors. *Larkin Oak*, a book compiled by Marcy and Walter Ayars, shows furniture given as premiums by the Larkin Soap Company. When no label was found on a sewing desk that a dealer called a Larkin, this helpful book was consulted. A desk pictured on page 11 has the same characteristics as the one that was photographed and included in this chapter. The 1901 catalog identifies it as a *Lady's Chautauqua Sewing Desk. Typewriter Desk* and *China Painter's Cabinet* were two other names given to the desk.

A desk four inches higher than the one just mentioned (with drawers opening at the left end as a storage section for medical instruments) was listed as a physician's special. Three hundred and fifty pleased physicians have ordered them for use in their offices, according to the Larkin catalogue.

Roll-top desks with an *S* curve sell better than those with a *C* curve. A desk of the former type has a tambour pull-down curtain on the left side and drawers to the right.

Fourteen-drawer file cabinet; 33" wide, 25" deep at base, 62" high. In Iowa, $750.

Sectional bookcase; 34" wide, 11" deep, 61" high. In Wisconsin, $650.

In the pictured example, a retractable shelf is present. The July 22, 1902 and April 30, 1907 patent dates listed on a metal plaque indicate that the desk was made after the last date. An additional brass plate states that this piece originated in Decatur, Illinois.

Combination double bookcase-desk with convex glass doors, beveled mirror, applied decorations, and grotesque above mirror; 55" wide, 13" deep, 73" high. In Indiana, $1,475.

Macey sectional bookcase; 34" wide, 12" deep, 49" high. In Indiana, $515.

Bookcase with pressed carving; 43" wide, 12" deep, 48" high. In Wisconsin, $550.

Combination bookcase-desk with beveled mirror and applied decorations; 38" wide, 12" deep, 68" high. In Illinois, $450.

Combination bookcase-desk with beveled mirror and applied decorations; 45" wide, 14" deep, 75" high. In Wisconsin, $1,395.

Fall-front parlor desk with applied decorations, beading in door panel, and mirrored storage compartment; 34" wide, 16" deep, 69" high. In Kentucky, $950.

Combination bookcase-desk with convex glass door, beveled mirror, applied decorations, pressed carving, and paw feet; 36" wide, 11" deep, 71" high. In Illinois, $675.

Ornately-carved fall-front desk with Man-of-the-Wind designs on drop lid and drawer fronts; 36" wide, 24" deep, 49" high; In Illinois, $1,575.

Fall-front desk with quarter-sawed veneered lid and fretwork on glass doors; 30" wide, 15" deep, 42" high. In Illinois, $265.

Fall-front desk with applied decorations and double-door storage compartment beneath fall-front; 32" wide, 14" deep, 45" high. In Wisconsin, $360.

Fall-front ladies' desk with beveled mirror and applied decorations; 30" wide, 17" deep, 51" high. In Illinois, $385.

Quarter-sawed oak fall front parlor desk; 32" wide, 16" deep, 47" high. In Kentucky, $300.

Fall-front parlor desk with storage compartments above and beneath drop lid; 28" wide, 15" deep, 62" high. In Iowa, $445.

Globe-Wernicke sectional bookcase made in Cincinnati, Ohio; 34" wide, 10" deep. 62" high. In Iowa, $595.

S-roll-top desk; 42" wide, 30" deep, 46" high. In Iowa, $795.

Combination bookcase-desk with convex glass door, beveled mirror, swell drawer beneath drop lid, applied decorations, and pressed carving; 37" wide, 11" deep, 72" high. In Wisconsin, $985.

Ash fall-front secretary with applied decorations and beading; 36" wide, 19" deep, 85" high. In Iowa, $1,295.

Quarter-sawed oak table desk with Queen Anne legs; 41" wide, 21" deep, 32" high. In Illinois, $475.

Combination bookcase-desk with convex glass door, and applied and incised decorations; 37" wide, 11" deep, 71" high. In Iowa, $650.

Fall-front secretary with incised and applied decorations; 35" wide, 18" deep, 78" high. In Illinois, $675.

Child's C-roll-top desk; 24" wide, 17" deep, 35" high. In Illinois, $120.

9
Accessories and Nonfurniture Items in Contemporary Homes

Plate rails, teacarts, clocks, telephones, and adopted occupational items.

Did You Know?

☐ *Thomas Edison's* favorite invention—out of his 1100 patented items—was the phonograph, which uttered its first words in 1877.

☐ *Clockmaker Eli Terry* developed machines in 1807 to make interchangeable parts for clocks. This development helped start the concept of mass production and assembly lines as used in modern factories. Prior to this, each clock was handcrafted individually.

☐ *Pendulums* should always be removed when transporting a clock to prevent possible damage to the mechanism. Weights on weight clocks should be removed, too, so that they do not damage the case or glass doors.

☐ An *eight-day clock* tends to sell better than those requiring daily winding. It's less time-consuming and more convenient to care for a clock only once a week.

☐ A *clockmaker* customarily pasted a paper label with his name on it either inside or on the back of the clock's case. The information may give evidence of the age of the clock.

☐ *Connecticut clockmakers* included their firm's names on their clocks. Massachusetts makers usually did not. This makes it difficult to attribute workmanship or

Edison Standard Phonograph with blue morning-glory horn, patented May 31, 1898, Orange, New Jersey; 12" wide, 9" deep, 12" high with cover on; horn 17" diameter. In Indiana, $495.

dates to the latter.

☐ A *regulator clock* was the name given to any wall clock that kept accurate time.

☐ *A practical sewing machine* was invented by Elias Howe in 1845.

☐ *Barbers' back bars* and *fireplace mantels* are two items that are classified as architectural antiques.

☐ The *Railroad Era* in the United States began with the opening of the Baltimore and Ohio and the South Carolina Railroads in 1830.

"What accessory articles are available to use with oak?" is an often-asked question. While some of the items illustrated in this chapter are not actually furniture that was originally intended to be used in the home, these items do add distinctive touches to the oak decor. A very battered and much consulted *The Encyclopedia of Furniture* (a classic in the field), by Joseph Aronson, contains, in addition to furniture, some nonfurniture selections. A few examples include an architect's table, clocks, and a knife box. As you peruse the chapter, enjoy the oak pieces with decorative possibilities.

In 1844, in his premiere telegraph message, Samuel F.B. Morse expressed his wonder as he typed out the words, "What hath God wrought?" In 1876, Alexander Graham Bell's original conversation by means of telephone was expressed out of need when he accidentally spilled acid on his clothes. "Mr. Watson, come here. I want you," was his plea for assistance. Bell learned that his invention worked because Watson was in another room and responded to his call immediately. These first words from the inventors on their new communications devices were unique.

In 1877, Thomas A. Edison was excited and delighted when a tinfoil covered cylinder repeated the nursery rhyme, "Mary had a little lamb," after the inventor recited this verse into a mouthpiece. That embryonic record captured the human voice, and out of all of his over 1100 inventions, the phonograph was Edison's favorite. Undoubtedly, another person was pleased when she heard the news. After all, Sarah Josepha Hale, pioneering editor of the trendsetting *Godey's Lady's Book*, composed the unpretentious story-poem to amuse her children, not to have it quoted at such an auspicious event.

Following that brief beginning, a new industry evolved as various companies based their new "talking machines" on Edison's phonograph. As the 1800s terminated, combination music box/phonographs, including the Reginaphone, were developed. By the early days of the new century, the phonograph was widely accepted. It pre-

Edison Gem Phonograph, patented October 3, 1905, Orange, New Jersey; 10" wide, 8" deep, 9" high with cover on. In Indiana, $395.

Ansonia schoolhouse clock manufactured by the Ansonia Clock Co., New York, circa 1878; 13" wide, 20" high. In Kentucky, $295.

served history by saving the voices of famous vocalists, authors, statesmen, and other illustrious leaders for future generations to hear. In addition, it was a fun machine, bringing happiness to its listeners.

Two Edison phonographs are illustrated. On one model, the sound is amplified by a large, blue, wooden morning glory horn with gold colored ribs.

Ansonia shelf or kitchen clock, patented March 1, 1881; 14" wide, 5" deep, 22" high. In Wisconsin, $225.

Another inventive man was Eli Terry. In 1807, this Connecticut clockmaker was undoubtedly considered crazy by his contemporaries when he contracted to produce the wooden works for 4000 clocks in three years. Because clocks were handmade to order, how could anyone promise to make thousands of them in such a short time?

In addition to the expensive craftsmanship, the brass works were handmade. Only affluent people could afford to own a clock. Terry changed all that. He developed machine tools to make inexpensive wooden parts that were identical and could be used interchangeably, and he harnessed waterpower to turn his lathes and wheel-cutting machines.

These ideas made mass production possible and reduced the cost of the movements. Eli Terry not only fullfilled his contract, but, by using the inexpensive wooden parts and

his quick production methods, he gave families with moderate incomes the opportunity to buy clocks. Terry's progressive ideas helped establish the American factory system.

These facts also indicate that wooden works in clocks are not necessarily older than hand-constructed brass examples. When a machine to stamp out metal parts was developed, brass works became inexpensive and were used once again.

Often there are clues to help date clocks. A clockmaker customarily pasted a paper containing his name (and oftentimes his location) either inside or outside on the back of the clock's case.

Books are available that indicate changes in companies' names and locations. For example, a firm established by Anson G. Phelps was located at Ansonia, Connecticut, from 1851–1878. It was moved to New York City and was in operation there from 1878–1930. If your label says New York City, your clock is from the latter period. Many collectors make every effort to preserve the labels on their clocks. Loose parts are reglued and sometimes a clear covering is placed over them.

Two Ansonia time pieces are pictured. The owner dates the miniature octagonal clock circa 1878 partly because its label reads, "Manufactured by the Ansonia Clock Co., New York, United States of America." As has been stated, the company did move to the Empire state in 1878. Another clue to its age is the style. Octagonal school clocks, which were often found on schoolhouse walls and in offices, and places of business as well, appeared in the 1870s. The case construction adds another clue—the gentle curving or *ogee* is an 1800s characteristic.

If a clock cannot hang on a wall or stand on the floor, it's referred to as a *shelf* or *mantel clock*. Some of these latter types served in kitchens and are designated as *kitchen clocks*. An Ansonia shelf clock with a pressed design on the wooden case is pictured. The patent date on the brass pendulum is March 1, 1881, which tells us that it was on the market in the late 1800s.

Ansonia octagonal school-type clock; 11" wide at base, 18" wide at top, 32" high. In Wisconsin, $450.

Regulator clock; 16" wide, 5" deep 32" high. In Kentucky, $295.

Various shelf, mantel, and kitchen clocks are illustrated. Their usage crossed the century line into the early 1900s. Notice that there are painted designs on the back of the glass on the doors of some of them. Even with the aid of stencils, this represents a tricky form of decorating. The design is executed in reverse on the back to come out in the correct position on the front.

Originally, falling weights were employed to make the wheels operate in a clock. It was difficult to prevent the weights from dropping too rapidly and to maintain a steady rate. By 1700, the pendulum was added and the problem was solved. While weights turned the wheels, the swinging pendulum started and stopped them. This caused revolutions with an even speed. The tick-tock sounds are caused as the escapement catches the wheel and releases it again.

The introduction of springs was an improvement. A main spring replaced the weights. Eventually, a balance wheel took the place of the pendulum to make the clock's wheels run evenly. However, clocks with pendulums are still produced.

Ingraham shelf clock; 15" wide, 5" deep, 23" high. In Wisconsin, $225.

Octagonal school-type clock; 12" wide, 4" deep, 23" high. In Tennessee, $175.

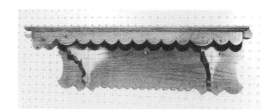

Clock shelf; 27" wide, 8" deep, 8" high. In Iowa, $55.

Walls are enhanced when they are decorated with antiques. In the late 1800s and early 1900s, *hangies* with a practical purpose were placed on the wall. For example, a kitchen clock needed a place to rest, so a wall shelf was provided.

Ingraham shelf clock; 15" wide, 5" deep, 22" high. In Wisconsin, $215.

Wall clock; 15" wide, 5" deep, 32" high. In Wisconsin, $395.

Clock shelf; 24" wide, 8" deep, 8" high. In Iowa, $55.

Shelf clock; 13" wide, 5" deep, 23" high. In Iowa, $225.

Shelf clock; 15" wide, 5" deep, 22" high. In Wisconsin, $225.

Comb holder with framed mirror and rings for towels. 14" wide, 3" deep, 24" high. In Indiana, $125.

Spice cabinet; 10" wide, 5" deep, 16" high. In Iowa, $110.

Wall pocket or comb case; 13" wide, 3" deep, 10" high. In Iowa, $45.

Plate rail, 34" wide, 24" high. In Iowa, $50.

If a family home had no inside water supply, someone pumped a pail of water and hauled it inside to use for drinking or washing purposes. Above the wash basin in the kitchen, a towel holder was needed. It could be separate, or part of a mirror/comb-case/towel-hanger combination.

When a housewife wanted to show off her prettiest floral plates, she arranged them in a plate rail. Another usual container was a spice cabinet that could either hang on a wall or stand on a shelf. Spices were available in bulk form so the housewife kept her cinnamon, cloves, nutmeg, ginger, and other spices in this handy box.

Most spice boxes bore applied or painted labels to indicate the contents of each drawer—but when a box is refinished, these generally are lost in the paint-removing process. Also, the constant exposure to

*Hanging hat box that was once part of a dresser;
12" wide, 11" deep, 38" high. In Iowa, $125.*

light, and the damp cloths used to clean
them has helped obscure the names. So
many of these cabinets are being made today
that if you want an old one, try following
your nose. A spicy odor may still be present
and vestiges of the old names may yet be
visible.

Since many spices are now purchased in
tins and are already ground, the spice boxes
are finding other places of employment.
Seamstresses like these boxes near their sewing machines to hold thread, buttons, snaps,
and other small sewing paraphernalia. Near
a desk, spice boxes can be used as organizers
for such things as stamps, paper clips, and
rubber bands.

*Wall telephone; 8" wide, 6" deep, 24" high. In Wis-
consin, $295.*

*Quarter-sawed-oak beveled wall mirror with ap-
plied decorations; 27" wide, 23" high. In Iowa,
$75.*

In 1876, only a year after its invention,
Alexander Graham Bell astonished visitors
at the Centennial Exposition in Philadelphia
by placing the telephone on exhibit. Years
later, long wooden cases held the working
parts of these wall telephones, and in some

142

Monarch wall telephone; 9" wide, 6" deep, 26" high. In Wisconsin, $285.

Oak frame with composition molding; 27" wide, 24" high. In Tennessee, $67.50.

rural areas, these were not removed from service until the late 1940s or early 1950s. A true collector likes to find a telephone with all its works intact. Some are gutted to hold a modern telephone or radio. Others simply hang around as novelties or conversational pieces.

Easel with oil landscape; 27" wide, 99" high. In Kentucky, easel $275; landscape $350.

Included under the heading of *architectural antiques* are fireplace mantels retrieved from gracious old homes that are being demolished. Examples shown feature varied decorative techniques. One has a removable cornice with applied decorations. Its pillars are highly carved and incised work is included.

As a part of another mantel, the fireplace is framed with green floral tiles, except for the top two that are the heads of a woman on the left and a man on the right. These reminders of the past are finding their way into new homes, theme restaurants, and other edifices.

Who would ever think that a treadle sewing machine would be collectible? While numerous men worked to develop a sewing machine and were successful, it was Elias

Fireplace mantel with beveled mirror, applied decorations, incised carvings, and four pillars supporting the cornice; 62" wide, 103" high. In Indiana, $1,895.

Singer sewing machine with carvings on doors and applied decorations; 36" wide, 18" deep, 30" high. In Iowa, $75.

Fireplace mantel with applied carving and green tiles framing hearth opening; 60" wide, 12" deep, 46" high. In Indiana, $1,200.

Quarter-sawed oak sewing machine cabinet with applied decorations; 22" wide, 18" deep, 30" high. In Illinois, $225.

The Eldridge sewing machine cabinet with oval incised designs on front and sides, and applied decorations; 26" wide, 20" deep, 34" high. In Illinois, $225.

Bobsled; 45" long, 16" wide, 12" high. In Tennessee, $260.

Tobacco truck used in warehouse to carry two baskets of tobacco, 38" square by 5" deep. Truck measures 85" wide, 35" deep, 22" high. In Tennessee, $255.

Howe who invented a practical type in 1845. His patent brought him wealth.

Isaac Singer added improvements, including a foot treadle. The cases became fancy, and the heads had painted designs on them. Some people remove the machine part, and by adding a marble slab or wooden top to the metal base, it becomes a table. The drawers are sometimes converted into small tables. Other people enjoy usable machines as is, or they electrify them.

Playthings from the past have a generous number of followers. Sleds with memories of scarf-bedecked children rushing down snowy hillsides may now live a passive life as magazine holders, coffee tables, or wall decorations.

What use can you find for a man-wheeled tobacco truck? In a large tobacco warehouse of the past, there might be over a hundred employees each assigned to push a hand truck about. These trucks held tobacco baskets made of interlaced wooden slats that were approximately 38 inches square and 5 inches high. Usually, two baskets of tobacco were carried on one of these trucks. Despite its hefty appearance, it was well balanced to push easily.

The persons in charge of these trucks were known by their vehicle numbers, not by their names. The wagon pictured came from Springfield, Tennessee and was operated by Mr. 130.

The tobacco truck's current use is varied. For example, it would be cheerfully bright if adorned with flowers, or imagine it in a store that sells women's apparel. How about a stack of sweaters on its surface? With the prevalence of country accents, it should add a nostalgic, charming touch to a decorating scheme.

Size creates problems for the use of the next item, although we have seen them in homes. A *barber's back bar* is considered an architectural antique. Four barbers had stations in the pictured back bar because there are that many stands beneath the continuous white-marble top. Only a portion of the

One section of a barber's back bar with white-marble top, two mirrors, and a station cabinet that measures 24" wide, 14" deep, 39" high. There are four such sections in the total back bar with a measurement of 15' 4" wide, 14" deep, 97" high. In Indiana, $6,500.

Store-counter desk and spool cabinet with lift-lid top; 30" wide, 22" deep, 17" high in back. In Wisconsin, $425.

Store-counter desk and spool cabinet with lift-lid top; 33" wide, 23" deep, 15" high. In Illinois, $425.

Spool cabinet; 21" wide, 15" deep, 15" high. In Wisconsin, $315.

piece could be photographed because of its size. If an individual cabinet is seen, it may have been a part of such a structure. Towels, clippers, scissors, brushes, perfumed skin lotion and other associated necessities were stored within.

The metal bases from inoperative sewing machines can be used to hold the desks that used to sit on the counters of yesterday's general stores. These lift-lid desks with ink wells and ridges for pencils were supplied to merchants, as storage places to keep the thread companys' products.

The counter desk was also an advertisement for the company who supplied them, since the company's name was printed on them. This was a reminder to both the shopkeeper to stock that company's brand, and to the female customers to buy that particular brand.

When cases are refinished, the printed or script designs often disappear unless special care is taken to preserve them. Multidrawer spool cabinets serve as small side tables, and the smaller ones function as organizers for jewelry, belts, or scarves on dresser

J. & P. Coats spool cabinet; 21" wide, 15" deep, 8" high. In Illinois, $270.

Coats and Clark spool cabinet; 21" wide, 25" deep, 23" high. In Kentucky, $395.

Railroad map case and table base. The four pull-out drawers contain maps of Tennessee, Georgia, Mississippi, and Arkansas; 29" wide, 22" deep, 31" high. In Tennessee, $255.

One-half section of a Corticelli double-spool cabinet with one side replaced; 23" wide, 17" deep, 32" high. In Iowa, $525.

Church pew with oak sides and back, and an elm seat; 50" wide, 33" high. In Illinois, $385.

tops. The Coats and Clark Company like the letters O.N.T. which deciphers to *Our New Thread.*

Even half of a Corticelli Silk and Twist thread cabinet is usable. A dealer assures customers that one side has been replaced and that there are new handles. If customers want to see what a full-sized one looks like, the dealer has them consult page 101 in Swedberg's *American Oak Furniture Styles and Prices*, the first book in the oak series.

Railroad lore is enticing. In the United States, the railroad era really began with the opening of the Baltimore and Ohio and the South Carolina railroads in 1830. In 1841, William Henry Harrison was the first President-elect to reach Washington, D.C. by rail. To get to the inaugural ceremonies, he traveled by means of a Baltimore and Ohio train.

Since the very first train tracks were laid across the American continent, there have been train enthusiasts. Today, railroad memorabilia is avidly collected by similar devotees.

The illustrated two-piece case holds railroad maps of Tennessee, Georgia, Mississippi, and Arkansas, respectively, in its four top-to-bottom drawers. No copyright date was found, but when one map was extracted and examined, it read "The Rand-McNally New Commercial Atlas of Tennessee." The map showed the state capital, county seats, and connecting railroad lines throughout the state. There is one drawer in the separate base table.

Church benches that no longer serve worshipping congregations have new places as benches in homes and business waiting rooms. Some of the smaller varieties may have been retrieved from choir lofts, while the larger ones have been cut down to adapt them for home use.

While accessory items and articles adopted from occupations are not actually furniture, modern homemakers enjoy their innovative appearance. Besides, not everybody on the block has a similar one, and they serve as conversation starters. In addition, they alert visitors to the creative possibilities of decorating with objects that combine heritage and history in a home setting.

10
The Arts and Crafts Movement

England's Ruskin, Morris, and Eastlake; Mission Furniture; the Stickleys; the Hubbards; Larkin; the Roycrofters; and Limbert.

Did you know?

☐ The *Eastlake style* of furniture originated when Charles Locke Eastlake began designing *rectilinear* furniture. He disliked the overly ornamental, massive curved examples that were shoddily produced by machine labor in the last half of the 1800s.

☐ The *Arts and Crafts Movement* began in England around 1875. Its idealistic leaders rebelled against the results of cheap machine workmanship in furniture making and other industries. Instead, they stressed the pride laborers feel through creating quality-made, handcrafted articles. Among the men who advocated, wrote about, and promoted these ideas were John Ruskin and William Morris. Their influence spread to the United States in the late 1800s.

☐ The *Roycroft Shop*, a colony for artisans, was established by Elbert Hubbard at East Aurora, New York, in 1895. Hubbard created the colony after visiting England and being influenced by leaders of the Arts and Crafts Movement.

☐ *Gustav Stickley* sailed to England in 1898. He was impressed by the teaching of the Arts and Crafts Movement and returned to the United States to experiment until he created structurally sound, plain-lined, functional furniture. This furniture became known as the *mission style*.

Eastlake cane-seat chair with burl strip on back rail; 36" high. In Wisconsin, $58.

☐ *Mission furniture* is the generic term for all the solid, straight, stoic oak furniture that was manufactured during the first part of the twentieth century. It became popular at the start of the twentieth century and began to lose its appeal around 1917.

Many companies throughout the country produced this furniture, and much of it was not quality crafted, but instead, retailed at an inexpensive price that the general public could afford to pay.

☐ *L. & J.G. Stickley,* Gustav's younger brothers, produced a quality line of mission furniture, which they marketed under the name *Handcraft.*

☐ *Quaint Furniture,* mission style, was produced by the Stickley Bros. Co., of Grand Rapids, Michigan. Another sibling, Albert, headed this enterprise.

☐ *Charles P. Limbert* of Grand Rapids and Holland, Michigan made quality mission furniture from 1903 to 1917 and called it *Art Crafts Furniture.*

☐ A *corbel* is a bracket or brace that is fastened to the leg of an arm chair, directly beneath and attached to the arms as a support. It serves a like function on tables and desks to brace their tops.

☐ A *key* is a small wedge-shaped piece of wood that is inserted through a slot in an exposed tenon to add strength as well as decoration.

☐ *Pins, pegs, or plugs* are round rods or dowels used to hold a mortise and tenon joint together.

☐ *Muntins* are light-weight, slender strips of wood that serve as dividers on the glass door of a piece of furniture. They can run either horizontally or vertically.

In what way did Charles Locke Eastlake (1836–1906) change home interiors? Because this English architect thought furnishings should be compatible with a house's physical structure, he designed furniture for homes he built. Eastlake felt curves were uncomfortable, wasted wood, and were not structurally strong. To him, straight lines were best. He did not desire to do away with factories just because they turned out so much inferior

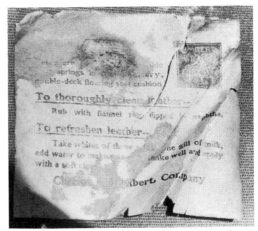

A Limbert label found on the bottom of a chair's seat cushion.

Eastlake elm dining room table with three leaves in place measures 75" wide, 42" deep, 29" high. In Wisconsin, $990.

work. Instead, he sought to show that well-designed furniture could be produced with the aid of machines. He liked simple squares and rectangles. Some of this boxy furniture, often of oak, had the wide boards, plain paneling, and large, primitive hardware inspired by early Gothic craftsmanship.

In an attempt to share his designs with others, he wrote a book with an impressive title, *Hints on Household Taste, Furnishings, Upholstery and Other Details.* It circulated

Morris-style recliner chair; 31" arm to arm, 35" high. In Kentucky, $140.

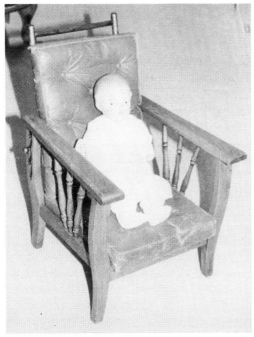

Child's Morris-style recliner chair with a movable metal rod that controls the reclining angle; 18" arm to arm, 26" high. In Wisconsin, $225.

widely around 1868. Through these written words and illustrations, many United States factory executives became impressed by Eastlake's straight line, but nevertheless, they seemed to derive pleasure from distorting his box-look. Chip carving, parallel incised lines (now called *railroad tracks*), and added appendages distorted the Englishman's plain furniture. Despite this, he did start the trend toward going straight.

On the other hand, John Ruskin (1819–1900) and William Morris (1834–1896) both were social reformers and crusaders who sought to promote a revival of interest in individual craftsmanship. The affluent university professor, John Ruskin, dedicated a portion of his inherited money to aid impoverished people. In addition, he and Morris both believed factory workers who operated machinery on a daily basis could not take delight in their work or achieve a sense of dignity through it. Ruskin wanted to get back to the basics and forget the machines and mass-produced factory outputs. He felt men should return to handcraftsmanship and take pride in their useful, cheerful, honest labor.

William Morris and John Ruskin felt that a home should contain only what was utilitarian or beautiful and promote the moral well being of its occupants. Morris and his followers disliked the overly ornate house interiors that resulted when the furniture manufacturers of their time borrowed motifs and styles from previous periods and mixed them haphazardly. They advocated doing away with this eclectic trend through the promotion of consciously designed furniture with cleaner, plainer lines.

Morris was also concerned with improving the lives of the laboring class who worked under deplorable conditions. He wanted men to find their jobs rewarding. If art could be a part of industry, men could achieve a sense of dignity from doing their tasks well.

Morris and some of his associates exchanged ideas. Why not establish a medieval guild-like situation where artisans could experience the joy of being creative while completing whole projects—rather than merely making machined parts and pieces as they did in factories?

In 1861, these men established a company in which products such as stained-glass windows, murals, tapestries, wood carvings, and simple furniture could be made. Book binding and metal work were also included. The accent was on individual artistry.

But the general public did not widely embrace this Arts and Crafts movement that seemed to turn back time. The Industrial Revolution (with its factory system) created new jobs and a new class of workers—namely, the middle class.

Mass production reduced the cost of many items that only the affluent class could previously afford. The middle class enjoyed this opportunity to buy products. However, some of the concepts of the Arts and Crafts advocates were adopted, as decorators began to replace cluttered interiors with an orderly, utilitarian appearance.

Ironically, William Morris's name became well known for another reason. He is credited with designing a recliner (called a Morris chair) that was copied repeatedly. In this chair, an adjustable rod enabled the sitter to change the degree of incline desired. An adult and a child's version are pictured.

Meanwhile, in a corresponding time period in the United States, John D. Larkin established a company in 1875 in Buffalo, New York that became the Larkin Soap Manufacturing Company in 1892. It sold hundreds of products directly to customers by mail, which eliminated the cost of the middleman. Larkin's brother-in-law, Elbert Hubbard (1856–1915), an author with a flamboyant personality, handled the advertising. Today's party plans—where products such as toys, jewelry, beauty, and cleaning supplies are sold to guests—might be based on the club ideas he promoted. When members bought Larkin products, they received free premiums equal in value

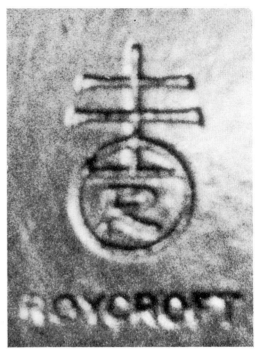

The Roycroft symbol found on the base of a brass jardeniere.

to the price of the product. For examples of the awards, look under Larkin in the index.

Hubbard left the Larkin Company after he visited England in the early 1890s, where he was inspired by William Morris' artisans at work. The Arts and Crafts Movement was compatible with his own ideas. He decided to create a similar colony of craftsmen, and his Roycroft Shop, established in 1895 in East Aurora, New York, was based on Morris's plan.

Roycroft products were marked with an orb and a cross, a symbol of royal power. The name in script was an identifying mark, too, and it was usually placed on furniture, even on the fronts of pieces, where it could be readily seen. Both the Larkin Club Plan and the Roycrofters outlasted Hubbard. He and his wife were among the over 100 American passengers who perished in 1915 when a German submarine sank the unarmed S.S. *Lusitania* in World War I.

Another man who espoused Arts and Crafts ideals was Gustav Stickley (1857–1942). Since he was born in a small Minne-

Gustav Stickley #354A V-back armchair, 26" arm to arm, 36" high; #354 V-back side chair, 36" high. In Missouri, a set of two arm chairs and four side chairs, $3,000.

sota town and was the oldest of five boys, he was accustomed to helping with the chores. Later, when the family had to get along without a father, he went to work for an uncle who ran a chair factory in Brandt, New York. From this early training, Stickley learned about wood working and how to perform assigned tasks well.

The first furniture he marketed (between the 1880s and the early 1890s) was the typical late 1800s ornate walnut style with fancy carvings. By the mid-1890s, he and a partner were manufacturing reproduction Chippendale pieces in Syracuse, New York.

Stickley visited England in 1898, and after he felt the impact of the Arts and Crafts advocates there, his past furniture-making ventures were forgotten. He returned home and experimented for two years to create the Craftsman furniture that was built in a strong, utilitarian style.

Stickley's wood preference was oak. The resulting products were exhibited at the Grand Rapids Furniture Exposition in 1900. His efforts were looked upon with favor, and soon, many companies were manufacturing this plain, strong, functional furniture.

It is doubtful that Gustav Stickley realized critics of the future would proclaim that he had created a truly new style of American furniture. However, that's exactly what happened. It's interesting to read about the leaders of the Arts and Crafts Movement in the

World Book Encyclopedia, published in 1936 by W. F. Quarrie & Company, Chicago. Gustav Stickley is not mentioned. Instead, Elbert Hubbard and his Roycrofters are included. Today Stickley is recognized as the leading exponent of the Arts and Crafts Movement in America.

Stickley chose Craftsman as the name for his furniture. How disappointing it was for him when the generic term *mission* was selected for this new style.

Various reasons were given for this choice. A common version said that the furniture resembled the plainly constructed forms found in the mission churches in the Southwestern United States. Manufacturers at times used cut-out or applied crosses on their pieces to emphasize this origin. Others thought furniture should meet a specific purpose. A chair's mission was to provide a place to sit. A desk was a space where a student worked. Each piece fullfilled its mission, its reason for being. That's how the term came into being. Some knowledgeable manufacturers realized *mission* was an outgrowth of the English Arts and Crafts Movement and, as Stickley did, worked that thought into their logos—but mission was the name that survived.

Stickley's's furniture evolved naturally as he continued to design his chairs, tables, and case pieces. It is thought that his contemporary, the British architect Baillie Scott, inspired some of his work. As an example, notice the arrangement of the stretchers on the two chairs in the illustration. There is a broad one at both the front and the rear while two slimmer, flat rungs are at each side. Baillie Scott produced chairs with a similar base structure. Further comparisons of the works of both men appear to add substance to the belief that Scott influenced Stickley.

Other points to notice on these chairs are the round rails that indicate the seats were made of rush, which Stickley frequently referred to as *raffia*. This type of seat represents one of his earlier styles. Observe, also, that on each chair, the top rail dips in the middle. He considered this slight *V* shape

Unmarked arm rocker with hard leather seat and an outline where the tag was; 26" arm to arm, 39" high. Gustav Stickley #305½ sewing rocker with leather seat and burnt-in joiner's mark; 17" wide, 31" high. In Iowa, arm rocker $175 and sewing rocker $275.

Unmarked Gustav Stickley-style rocker on the left with a replaced leather seat; 28" arm to arm, 34" high. Limbert rocker on the right with branded mark under the arm; 27" arm to arm, 32" high. In South Dakota, unmarked Stickley style $175 and Limbert $175.

one of his favorite designs, and he used it on a high billiard chair as well as on a rocker. As is noted under the pictures, these chairs are a part of a set of four side chairs and two arm chairs. The inclusion of arm chairs adds to the value of a set.

Stickley hunters use original as well as reissued catalogs to try to trace unmarked articles. They become detectives as they turn the pages to check for similar sizes and styles. They also take a tally of typical Stickley construction details. Here are some characteristics as seen on the unmarked arm rocker in the illustration to the left, attributed to Gustav Stickley. The ornamental tacks that he liked had an almost pyramid-shaped head. He, as well as others, used a corbel. The typical Stickley pins or wooden pegs that hold a mortise and tenon joint together are there, but don't show up well in the photograph.

If there's an outline where a tag once went, the detectives inspect that, too, to determine which of the various-sized labels would fit the mark. Even though all other indications may point to Stickley, a bona fide label gives any piece positive identification. The sewing rocker on the right meets this latter qualification. It has the black burnt-in joiner's compass and is listed as number 305½ in the catalog. Both rockers have original leather on their cushions.

Limbert rocker with brown leather seat and added upholstery pad on the back; 27" arm to arm, 33" high. In Iowa, $50 at auction.

Gustav Stickley #225 even-arm settle without the spring-cushion seat; 78" wide, 31" deep, 29" high. In Minnesota, $6,000.

154

Stickely Brothers #3752 Quaint youth or day bed. In Iowa, $750.

Gustav Stickley dining room table and chairs; table 48" x 63", 30" high; master or host chair, 20" arm to arm, 38" high; side chairs, 34" high. In Nebraska, the nine-piece set including table, 6 chairs, a sideboard and a china cabinet, $9,500.

Dealers point out that because ordinary rocking chairs are more readily available than other mission furniture, they generally do not cost as much as other pieces.

Two rockers were photographed. The one to the left is unmarked but done in the Stickley manner. The cushion cover has been replaced. On the right-hand side is a Charles Limbert creation. The company's branded trade mark, which was used from 1903 to 1917, the time span during which Limbert made mission furniture, is under the arm. The corbels on each chair are easily seen.

An even-arm *settle* with the black-branded joiner's compass and Gustav Stickley's signature has been known to sell at auction for over $6,000. The photograph clearly shows the exposed tenons that extend beyond the surface—a decorative device used by Stickley.

A more valuable variation of an even-arm settle is a knock-down version. Only two or three examples are known to exist.

Couches in the Stickley style differ from settles. They're generally backless while settles have backs in most cases.

Seven pieces of a nine-piece Gustav Stickley dining room set are illustrated. The master chair was designed with sinking arms to enable it to be drawn closer to the table without crowding. The other pieces not included in the photograph are a china cabinet and a sideboard.

The Craftsman, a magazine put out by Gustav Stickley, introduced the china cabinet in its November, 1914 issue. A fabric with a suede feel was applied on the inside back of the cabinet. The dealer who owns this set said that in order to maintain its maximum value, the suit should not be split up.

It's both educational and entertaining to browse through copies of *The Craftsman*. Through this magazine, Stickley presented his philosophies and promoted the Arts and Crafts Movement's beliefs. He invited and encouraged people who liked to do handwork to send for his patterns. They could purchase his hardware so that necessary handles and hinges would be authentic. Leather was available. Fabrics, some of which were stamped to be embroidered, could be secured through this magazine. Because he wanted to promote home arts and crafts, the fact that he might be cutting into his own sales by letting everyone use his patterns did not seem to disturb him. What did annoy him, however, were his professional competitors.

Stickley's vexing problem was how to prevent his Craftsman furniture from being confused with inferior products produced by other companies. The superior quality of his workmanship should have been sufficient to separate his offering from theirs, but names and symbols similar to his patented Craftsman name and his joiner's compass appeared. He thought that if he increased the size of his decals and applied his burnt-in stamp, the distinction would be immediately obvious. A dining room suit composed of six chairs (of which only four are pictured), an extension table, and a sideboard have labels that differ from each other and show a slight variation in the years that the articles were first placed on the market.

The six ladder-back chairs (catalog #370) are marked with the early small red decal (1901–1903) with the compass and the maker's signature. Originally, the seats were rushed. Later, some chairs could be purchased with a choice of either a rush or a soft leather slip seat.

The quarter-sawed oak split-pedestal table, #656, with its large red decal, represents a later year. Yet another distinguishing mark, a burnt-in symbol on the side of the top drawers, is on the #814½ buffet. An ooze leather lines the drawer, and the hand-hammered copper hardware adds a distinctive quality touch. There is a slight crest on the sideboard's back rail, and in addition, there is a plate rail.

Since items were carried over from one catalog to another, it was possible to purchase older pieces along with those that had been recently introduced.

Two of Gustav Stickley's emulators especially irked him—because they bore his family name. The factory his younger brothers Leopold and J. George started in 1902 in Fayetteville, New York, not too many miles from their big brother's establishment, was called The Onondago Shops.

The brothers announced a line of "Simple Furniture Built on a Mission Line" under their Onondago label. The quality of their workmanship and designs, plus J. George's inordinate ability as a salesman, combined to bring them rapid success. When, in 1910, their logo changed to show a joiner's wooden clamp combined with L & J.G. Stickley and the name "Handcraft," it very closely resembled Gustav Stickley's compass and Craftsman title for his furniture.

Gustav Stickley #656 split-pedestal table that extends to 12 feet has a large red decal label; 54" diameter, 29" high. #370 ladder-back chairs that have small red decal labels; 36" high. #814½ sideboard with ooze leather in the top drawer and a burnt-in mark on the drawer's side; 56" wide, 21" deep, 48" high. In Minnesota, table $2,250; ladder-back chairs, $1,200 for six; sideboard, $1,500.

Gustav Stickley #636 Ellis-inspired game table with arched apron and stretchers; 48" diameter, 30" high. In Minnesota, $1,200.

Sharing the same last name provided additional confusion for the public. Fortunately, the little brothers adopted a new decal in 1912. Within a simple rectangle were the words "The work of L & J.G. Stickley." With this change, the similarities in the labels of the two companies ceased to exist.

L & J.G. Stickley #530 Handcraft one-drawer table; 48" wide, 30" deep, 30" high. In Iowa, $475.

Stickley Brothers #2570 Quaint table; 40" wide, 26" deep, 30" high. In South Dakota, $225.

The mark, used from 1910 to 1912, that was found on the L & J.G. Stickly table from Iowa.

The decal and the burnt-in labels found on the Quaint table from South Dakota.

There were other imitators that Gustav Stickley mentioned in *The Craftsman* magazine. He felt their brand names were too close to his own. His list included *Roycroft, Hand-Craft, Arts and Crafts, Crafts-Style* and his brother Albert's *Quaint Furniture.*

He promised customers they could return work found unsatisfactory. He strived to be the best. It is said that he once became angry when one of his workmen did not complete a furniture project to meet his standards of quality. Contemptuously, he destroyed it. Because of this constant desire to do well, it's not strange he disliked emulators, some of whom were not as attentive to details as was he.

It did seem as if his brothers L & J.G. copied Craftsman styles, but they were also capable of producing well-designed works on their own. As an example, the furniture they made for smaller and larger persons demonstrated that they could produce pieces that met individual needs.

A Handcraft brand one-drawer table with hammered metal drawer handles appears in a photograph. The boards on the top are butted together, and visible splines help hold them in place. It's easy to see the tenons, which serve as both a joining and decorating feature, projecting through the legs. The keys in the shelf tenons add further interest.

The label found on the table is from the 1910–1912 period. It's interesting to note that the L & J.G. Stickley Company remains in existence today.

After his siblings departed from furniture interests in Michigan, Albert Stickley was left to head Stickley Bros. of Grand Rapids. A table that is marked with both the Quaint decal and the branded Stickley Bros. Co. is illustrated, along with a picture of the trademarks.

Some of the techniques Gustav Stickley employed will be briefly discussed. Except for one other person, Gustav Stickley created his own furniture and did not employ designers. That one man was Harvey Ellis, a talented architect who designed some Stickley furniture from 1903 until his untimely death in 1904. He added a gentle touch to stoic Stickley pieces. An arched apron on cupboards, bookcases, sideboards, or china cabinets was his influence. Ellis liked inlay work, and these designs on chair backs added a delicate look.

While some inlaid furniture was exhibited, it never proved to be popular. Pieces with Ellis arched aprons were produced, however, so his influence was felt.

For Stickley's fumed oak finish, refer to Chapter 1.

Stickley rejected the glittering, lacy, fragile, metal hardware that served as handles or escutcheons on golden oak furniture. Instead, he designed plain iron and copper hand-hammered handles, and exaggerated hinges and escutcheons that were darkened to give them an old look. The resulting hardware complimented the severe, straight lines of his furniture. At times, however, plain wooden knobs were also used.

The 1910 Craftsman Furniture Catalog announced that the rockers currently in use on chairs were cut straight with the grain of the wood and bent into shape by machine. This made them stronger than those that were cut on a curve so that a portion crossed the grain. The latter tended to break more easily than the former.

A *joiner* is one who joins together pieces of wood in the construction of furniture. Traditionally, he used wooden dowels, mortise, and tenons or other devices to hold parts together without the aid of glue or metal (including nails and screws). Stickley copied these techniques both as joining devices and as a way to create decorative effects. However, he was not opposed to the use of glue.

Some of his construction details are listed below, but it is important to note that other factories used similar techniques. Most of his rivals lacked his finesse, however.

The *mortise and tenon joint,* the *pins* (pegs) and the *keys* that held them together, the *corbel,* the *spline,* the *chamfering,* and the *cleats,* are all joiners' techniques that are defined in the glossary.

Stickley united two butt-joined boards on some early pieces of his furniture by chamfering their edges. He also chamfered the edges of the cleats he used on the under portion of tabletops or inside cabinet doors. These strips of wood provided strength and helped reduce warping.

Dealers who were interviewed listed certain Gustav Stickley pieces that are difficult to find. Among these are the even-arm settle that comes apart to transport, chairs with inlay work, and those with a series of spindles rather than the wider type of flat slats.

For a brief span in 1900, Stickley apparently did not mark his own furniture. The Tobey Furniture Company of Chicago marketed a line of *New Art Furniture* produced by Stickley. Their circular Toby label failed to include his name.

In 1901 the first logo devised by Gustav Stickley showed a joiner's compass, which enclosed his initials. Beneath it were the words *Als ik kan* (As I can) and *Gustav Stickley, Cabinet Maker, Syracuse, N. Y.* It is doubtful, however, whether this trademark was ever used on furniture.

After that, a new format developed and was used with variations throughout the years that Craftsman products were made. In 1902–1903, the motto, surrounded by the compass symbol and the maker's signature within a rectangle beneath it, appeared on furniture as a red decal.

Perhaps as a measure to keep the public from becoming confused with the works of the various Stickley-run companies, Gustav Stickley spelled out his entire name on his decal labels from 1904 to 1912. Usually in red, the trademark was expanded somewhat in size.

Search in unobtrusive places, such as inside drawers, on the rear stretchers of chairs, inside bookcases and china cabinets, and under table tops for this symbol.

From 1912 to 1916 a burnt-in trademark was in use. Except for the fact that Stickley returned to including only his last name, the branded mark resembled its predecessor. Various paper labels bearing the Craftsman name appeared separately but in conjunction with the trademark. Stickley felt his furniture was fine enough to rate an heirloom status and that families could treasure his work for generations to come. He predicted this furniture would increase vastly in price in the future.

After a revival of interest in the Arts and Crafts Movement occurred in the late 1960s and early 1970s, his prophetic statement came true. Thousands of dollars are now paid for certain Gustav Stickley pieces.

This man had so many plans. He bought extensive property and envisioned establishing a Morris-type colony where artisans could live and enjoy a creative, fruitful life.

Stickley never established his Arts and Crafts Movement–inspired haven. Instead he was forced to declare bankruptcy in 1916. It is necessary to speculate about the causes for his economic disaster. Perhaps he overextended himself by trying to build houses and coordinate their interiors with everything from lights, to accessories, to fabrics, to furniture. Maybe he helped discourage amateur woodworkers from buying his products by letting them purchase patterns.

Since inexpensive mission furniture was available from many companies, including mail-order houses, undoubtedly they took over a portion of his market. In addition—and against the advise of some who felt that people would not buy when nations were fighting (in what came to be called World War I)—Stickley invested heavily when he constructed an expensive Craftsman Building for his headquarters in New York City.

Stickley's advisers felt that sooner or later the United States would become involved in the hostilities. Besides all this, the public was losing interest in plain furniture, as a new design—the so-called *colonial style*—began to attract attention. Perhaps all of these factors combined to bring about the crash of the Craftsman enterprises. At any rate, Gustav Stickley's shops closed in 1916.

Except for a brief time when he joined his brothers in a united firm, the man whose work has been acclaimed as the forerunner of modern furniture, and who realized machines could help produce well-designed home furnishings, was no longer a member of the trade. It remained for future generations to appreciate both golden oak and mission furniture once again.

At the end of the chapter are pictures of pieces not associated with any special company and, as a consequence, the price drop is abrupt.

One piece deserves special comment. How unusual it is to open a section of a quarter-sawed oak mission desk to discover that a phonograph is concealed within. An examination of the desk shows that the long top drawer is a fake one that provides space for the wind up Columbia Regent phonograph and its horn amplifier. Two doors below afford storage space—one on either side of the knee hole.

Child's chair, 28" high. In Wisconsin, $30.

Columbia Regent desk phonograph; 46" wide, 29" deep, 31" high. On the top of the desk sits an Edison Amberola cylinder phonograph with 30 cylinders; 13" wide, 16" deep, 14" high. In Kentucky, Columbia Regent $795 and Edison $345.

Pedestal table with four leaves; 48" diameter, 31" high. In Illinois, $525.

Umbrella stand; 13" square, 30" high. In Illinois, $85.

Sewing rocker with drawer for supplies; 35" high. In Illinois, $95.

Library table; 41" wide, 26" deep, 29" high. In Wisconsin, $90.

Buffet; 60" wide, 23" deep, 56" high. In Illinois, $385.

If one music maker is not enough, a second, enclosed in an oak case, sits on top of the desk. It is an Edison Amberola cylinder phonograph with 30 cylinders.

Also perched atop the desk is a statue of Nipper, the pin-up pup of the cur kingdom who served as an advertising symbol for Victor Talking Machine Company. When RCA (Radio Corporation of America) took over Victor, Nipper tagged along. In a few more years, he'll be 100 years old.

Child's arm rocker; 19" arm to arm, 23" high. In Iowa, $55.

Bookcase with arched apron, similar to the type that Ellis used on Gustav Stickley furniture. In Wisconsin, $699.

Fall-front desk with open storage space above lower drawer; 28" wide, 15" deep, 40" high. In Iowa, $285.

Fall-front desk; 30" wide, 17" deep, 25" high. In Wisconsin, $285.

Fall-front desk; 30" wide, 17" deep, 25" high. In Wisconsin, $285 for both.

162

Child's fall-front desk; 23" wide, 13" deep, 43" high. In Kentucky, $159.

Hall tree, which came from a library, with seven iron coat-and-hat hooks and two umbrella holders with copper drip pans; 40" wide, 15" deep, 72" high. In Iowa, $380.

Lamp; 17" square shade, 27" high. In Wisconsin, $225.

Bibliography

Ayars, Marcy, and Walter Ayars. *Larkin Oak.* Summerdale: Echo Publishing, 1984.

Brown, Don. *Oak Furniture Styles and Prices.* Des Moines: Wallace-Homestead Book Co. 1975.

Cathers, David M. *Furniture of the American Arts and Crafts Movement Stickley and Roycroft Mission Oak.* New York: New American Library, 1981.

Hamilton, Charles F. *Roycroft Collectibles.* San Diego: A.S. Barnes & Company, Inc., 1980.

Hill, Conover. *Antique Oak Furniture.* Paducah: Collector Books, 1976.

Miller, Robert W. *Clock Guide Identification with Prices.* Des Moines: Wallace-Homestead Book Co., 1974.

Stickley, Gustav and L. & J. G. Stickley. *Stickley Craftsman Furniture Catalogs:* "Craftsman Furniture Made by Gustav Stickley" and "The Work of L. & J. G. Stickley." Introduction by David Cathers. New York: Dover Publications, Inc., 1979.

Swedberg, Robert W., and Harriett Swedberg. *Furniture of the Depression Era.* Paducah: Collector Books, 1987.

————. *American Oak Furniture Styles and Prices.* Des Moines: Wallace-Homestead Book Co., 1982.

————. *American Oak Furniture Styles and Prices, Book II.* Lombard: Wallace-Homestead Book Co., 1984.

Catalogues

Israel, Fred L., ed. *1897 Sears Roebuck Catalogue.* New York: Chelsea House Publishers, 1976.

Montgomery Ward & Co., Catalogue No. 99. Chicago: Fall and Winter 1923–1924.

Montgomery Ward & Co., Catalogue No. 110. Chicago: Spring and Summer 1929.

Sears, Roebuck and Co. Catalogue No. 154. Chicago: Spring and Summer 1927.

Schroeder, Joseph J., Jr., ed. *1908 Sears, Roebuck Catalogue.* Chicago: The Gun Digest Company, 1969.

————. *Sears, Roebuck and Co. Catalogue No. 110 Fall 1900.* Northfield: DBI Books, Inc. 1970.

Ward's Catalog for Spring and Summer No. 118. Chicago: 1933.

Periodicals

Koehler, Arthur. *The Identification of Furniture Woods, Circular No. 66.* Washington: United States Department of Agriculture, November 1926.

Glossary

Applied Decoration
An ornamentation crafted separately and applied to a piece of furniture.

Artificial Graining
Paint or stain applied to furniture to imitate the grain (figure) of a specific wood.

Atlantes
A supporting pillar designed in the form of a man.

Buffet
See *Sideboard.*

Cane
A long, narrow strip of rattan used for weaving chair seats and backs.

Caryatid
A supporting pillar designed in the form of a woman.

Cheval (Chevalle) Mirror
A tall mirror supported by an upright frame. A cheval dresser has a mirror of this type set to the side of the hat cabinet.

Chiffonier
A tall, narrow chest of drawers, often called a *highboy* by today's collectors.

Chifforobe
An article of furniture made with a chest of drawers on one side and a narrow wardrobe on the other.

Chimera (Chimaera)
A fire-breathing creature from Greek mythology, having a lion's head, a goat's body, and a serpent's tail. Generally, a horrible creature of the imagination.

Circa (C. or c.)
An approximate date used when the exact date is unknown. For example, sometime during the mid-1920s would be "circa 1925."

Claw Foot
Furniture feet that resemble the claws of a bird.

Closed Cupboard
A cupboard with glassless doors.

Commode
An enclosed, cupboard-type washstand, usually including one or more drawers or doors.

Concave
A surface that curves inwardly.

Convex
A surface that curves outwardly.

Crest
The carved piece on the top rail of a sofa or chair.

Divan
A small sofa.

Eclectic
In furniture design, the practice of borrowing, combining, or adapting previous styles in order to give latitude to a designer's creativity.

Extension Table
A table top that pulls apart so that leaves may be added to enlarge it.

Fall Front
A hinged lid on a desk that drops down to form a writing surface.

Finger Hold
A cut-out part in the back rail of a chair into which the fingers may be inserted to move the chair.

Finial
A carved, cast, or turned terminal ornament on furniture, clocks, or accessory pieces.

French Leg
A leg with a double curve flowing out at the knee, in at the ankle, and then slightly outward again.

Fretwork
An ornamental border that is perforated or cut in low relief. Often called *open lattice work.*

Griffin
An imaginary creature with the head, wing, and forelegs of an eagle, and the body, hind legs, and tail of a lion.

Grotesques
Figures, or parts of figures, of animals and people mixed with flowers, fruits, or foliage, created in a fantastic or unnatural way.

Highboy
New term for chiffonier.

Hoosier
Now, a generic name for a kitchen cabinet that has a pull-out work surface, meal or flour bins, drawers, sifters, cupboard space, and other features. This one-unit cabinet was made in the late 1800s and early 1900s in the Hoosier state (Indiana) and elsewhere.

Incised
A design cut or engraved into the surface.

Marriage
When pieces of furniture not originally intended to be united are combined as one, such as a bookcase top added to a fall-front desk in order to form a secretary.

Mullions
Narrow dividing bars between windowpanes or doors of bookcases, china cabinets, and other pieces with glass enclosures.

Ogee
A molding with a continuous double curve.

Open Lattice Work
Narrow crossed strips or bars of wood or metal used for decorative trim.

Plain-Sawed
Boards cut from the whole log, lengthwise, in parallel cuts. This results in a pattern of stripes and a series of eliptical *V*'s.

Pressed Back
A design pressed into the back of a chair with a metal die, to imitate carving. Pressed designs are also used on other pieces of furniture.

Projection Front
A top drawer that protrudes over the rest of the drawers, as seen in dressers and washstands.

Quarter-Sawed
Cutting a log into quarters by splitting it lengthwise and cutting each half into half, again. Each quarter is then cut into parallel boards at right angles to the annual growth rings. Although such cutting wastes wood, the resulting pattern vividly exposes the flakes or *pith rays* to produce a pronounced pattern.

Serpentine
A snakelike curve that is convex at the center and at both ends, and concave between.

Sideboard (Buffet)
A piece of furniture for storing silverware, dishes, linens, or other tableware in a dining area.

Slat
A horizontal crossbar in a chair back.

Splat
The center upright in a chair back.

Splay
Slanting out, as chair legs slant outward from the seat to the floor.

Spoon Carving
Decorative carving that resembles the bowl of a spoon.

Stile
The upright piece of a frame or panel in furniture.

Stretcher
The rung or cross piece that connects cabinet, table, or chair legs.

Swell Front
An old catalogue term synonymous with the word *convex*.

Taboret (Tabourette)
A small plant stand.

Veneer
A thin layer of decorative wood glued over the surface of another wood to add beauty to a piece.

Victorian
Furniture made during the reign of England's Queen Victoria (1837–1901). Much was machine made and overly ornamental.

Wardrobe
A piece of furniture in which clothes are hung.

Index

About the Authors

Bob and Harriett Swedberg travel thousands of miles when they research and write books, and they meet many fine people along the way who share their interest in preserving heritage articles for future generations. While they enjoy visiting museums, they do not include museum pieces in their books. The Swedbergs only photograph articles that are actually available to the public for purchase, or those that are in the possession of people who secure them to preserve or collect. To date, this couple has written books on oak, wicker, Country, Depression, and Victorian furniture, on advertising, and on refinishing and repairing antiques. The Swedbergs are available as speakers and enjoy teaching about America's heritage through antiques classes.